To: Rob

May this book
provide you
with Spiritual
Guidance + Blessings

God bless

Claudel Corcuera

A Butterfly Flies Towards the Wind

A Collection of Poems, Thoughts, and Memories in English and Spanish

By
Claribel Coreano

authorHOUSE™

1663 LIBERTY DRIVE, SUITE 200
BLOOMINGTON, INDIANA 47403
(800) 839-8640
WWW.AUTHORHOUSE.COM

AuthorHouse™
1663 Liberty Drive, Suite 200
Bloomington, IN 47403
www.authorhouse.com
Phone: 1-800-839-8640

AuthorHouse™ UK Ltd.
500 Avebury Boulevard
Central Milton Keynes, MK9 2BE
www.authorhouse.co.uk
Phone: 08001974150

First published by AuthorHouse 7/25/2006

ISBN: 1-4208-2868-1 (sc)

Printed in the United States of America
Bloomington, Indiana

This book is printed on acid-free paper.

Introduction

I began to write poems back in September 2003. This was when I wrote my first poem, then every other day I would sit down at my computer and write my thoughts down. I was experiencing a surge of ideas and thoughts coming to my mind frequently. Whenever this happened I would write them.

There was someone very special who inspired me to write, a special friend who taught me many things in a very short time. I dedicate this book to him. He knows who he is…. I have written many poems about him. He was my soul mate and spiritual guide, but he soon entered my life and quickly he disappeared. All I have left is the fond memories I have written of him; I will never forget him because I know he was my soul mate.

During this period in my life I had begun many changes. I was recently divorced and had moved to a new state to start a new life. I had gone through many personal experiences during this time and I started to write to vent my feelings. I had also begun a metamorphosis while writing which brought about many changes in my life.

When I first began writing this book, I had not yet experienced a personal relationship with God; therefore, some poems are sexual in context to some degree. I began to change some of my writing by the middle of my manuscript and I realized that yes, I am a new individual in Christ, and I automatically began writing in a more conscious style.

I decided to include these poems because I had written them already, and why exclude them from the book? I said to myself what better way to show how much my life has changed than to let others see the difference. I am in no way a writer; I am just a simple woman who has decided to share some thoughts with others in the hope that I can in some way inspire others spiritually or provide a motivation for change. I have gone through my share of pain and I hope that it has not been in vain, that I can somehow encourage other individuals who are going through similar experiences to come out of that cycle of abuse. My only hope is that they can get out in time. Yes, I experienced it and yes, I have survived. This is in fact my motivation to write and express my sentiment with words.

I vent to let go and release all the memories of these experiences. I hope that I can help others come out and see the light.

I have been very determined to finish this book of poems, but with a special purpose in mind; I wanted to find out that yes, I can do it. Someone as humble as I can write a book. If by chance I make some money from it, it will be for my goal in life, which is to build an orphanage in the Dominican Republic and to assist a homeless family shelter in the United States. This to me is a great reason to keep going and has motivated me to write even more. When I first began writing, my goal was to write 100 pages or more and thanks to God, I have surpassed my actual goal. I thank God for giving me the opportunity to complete this project and to achieve something positive as a result of my experiences. I thank God for the lessons in life I learned that have helped me become the assertive individual I am today. Once again I thank my Lord and Savior Jesus Christ.

By reading this simple book you will assist those in need. My sincerest gratitude from the heart. —Claribel

I thank God for my children and for blessing me with love, hope, and a future.
I love you Mom and Dad.
To my four sisters, who are also my best friends, and to my only brother, I love you all.

Searching...

Some individuals go through life searching for that "special milestone"
that they think will make them happy
or at least complete them in one way or another.
Some individuals depend on others to fulfill their emptiness;
others go through life feeling unfulfilled and never satisfied.
Some individuals substitute the void by using
money, drugs, or women/men to find a temporary high in life.
In contrast, I have lived my life like a caterpillar securely nested in a
cocoon
protected by my simplicity and unknowingness.
I can say I have lived this way until now.
Yet I have discovered myself and realize what I deserve in life.
Finally, I can say that I have changed as an individual
and have grown into a beautiful butterfly
that just recently got its wings, in search
of freedom and the happiness I deserve....
Claribel

Table of Contents

Women

How Do I Describe "Myself"?

Let me start by saying that I am a romantic at heart.
I was to be born in the Renaissance era instead of the sixties.
I have always been caring and loving,
Helping and thinking of others before myself.
When I was a child I kept a jar of pennies
which I collected to give to my father
for the poor children of the neighborhood.
I was a born social worker; I've listened to so many people's stories
Without asking for details.
Strangers have always told me everything about themselves
And often people share their problems
As if I can help.
I often wonder if it is a gift or a curse, because I only have to say hello
And instantly a counselor I become.
I hear that listening is a gift that not everyone acquires.
It is a talent to be able to be patient and just listen to others.
I see it every day in my job, where I go and I feel at times that I
Share my energy with others.
Love escapes from my heart to them
And allows them some comfort.

For I am not a wealthy woman, or a scholar, or even a famous person.
It's just that I've been given the ability to be patient listener.
From the wisdom that God gives me at that moment,
A kind word I can share,
Provide some guidance in all humbleness,
And for this I think I am blessed.
For who am I, I often question, to think I can help others?

But what better understanding is the wisdom God provides us,
That even though my life is not perfect
I am able to share with people who are in need.
It's a blessing to help others grow spiritually.
Wasn't that in fact what Jesus did and asks us to do?

In my heart I see a dream, a goal that has been placed,
That is to one day build an orphanage in my country
To provide a haven for many growing babies
Who have lost their parents through unfortunate means.
I will one day make this goal come true
For I know that it is in God's plan.

Woman

I am a woman, unique, beautiful, and wonderful.
My uniqueness comes from not being afraid to be me.
I speak my mind and tell the truth like it is.
Simple in my ways, no need to be sophisticated and vain,
Beautiful inside and out,
The light that shines inside my heart glows outside.
Goodness and purity is the energy of my soul.
Wonderful, for I am a good soul who respect others,
Who gives out of love, who knows how to love,
And who shares love with others.
I am different because I have made a pact with myself
that I will not give myself intimately in vain.
I learned many lessons in life of truth, knowledge, and awareness.
The good that is in me has made me to be trusting of others,
But I have been enlightened not to believe everything I am told.
To err is human.
We all make mistakes.
No one is perfect in this world.
Accept me as I am.
Don't try to figure me out.
You can't, you won't, and you would not understand.

I am strange in my ways, yes; it's hard to admit it,
But at least I know in what areas.
I know my own weakness.
I am not afraid to deal with it,
Confront myself,
Teach myself what I must change.
Accept the truth about me,
Work on things I must refine,
Mold my character.
My personality has already been there.
Loving nature.
Loving heart.
Caring individual.
I know myself to know what I deserve.
Don't try to deceive me by being contemptuous,
Because you are making a fool of yourself instead of me.

I am unique. I have learned that you need to give others respect,
Acknowledge their emotions, feelings, and what they are trying to say.
A woman so wonderful that I give the benefit of the doubt to allow you
To come around and tell the truth somehow.
My life is based on openness because I feel free
And do not have anything to hide.
If you ask me about me I will tell you the truth.
Yes, I did not have an easy life,
But I learned that being open in heart, mind, and soul
Makes you free and strong.
Am I interesting?
Yes, I must say!
I am very talented and creative in my lifestyle.
I like to see the beauty in any object I touch, feel,
see, or become acquainted with.
I am a vessel of peace and tranquility.
I love to teach others to maintain hope.
I live my life as an example of what I have accomplished.
I have been through many difficult experiences,
Many trials and tribulations,
But guess what?
I have come out on top!
I have survived as a woman.
I have made it!
I am an unique, wonderful, and beautiful woman,
For I am a woman of God.
That makes me even more interesting.
I am not afraid to say it,
That my belief in God has made me
Special in his eyes,
Valued by him,
Accepted by him,
And blessed to have been saved!

My Four Sons

JOSHUA
Born on a cold, winter evening,
your hair as black as coal,
fuzzy like a bear,
your red, round cheeks were the first things to notice
your long arms and legs made you look so funny—

A big baby you were,
hair style like Elvis
even though your skin was of olive complexion.

My firstborn,
you gave me a tough time,
fighting to stay in
when we wanted you outside.
You struggled for hours,
finally gave up then welcomed the world
with the loudest scream until the end of time.

Your temperament could be visible then;
you were going to be a screamer,
with no doubt you could hear.
I pity my middle ear—
You fussy baby that
needed attention all the time,
little did I know that you were a party child at heart.

I remember on your first birthday
with your pin-striped suit,
dressed like a Mafioso
you danced to every tune.
You were born to dance;
you had the music inside you.
It showed in your movements and rhythms.
I regret that I did not invest in your dancing feet,
but don't regret you are now a great kosher sous chef.

You were a smart cookie even as a child.
You liked to discuss sports statistics.
You knew every player's name,
where they were born,
how many hits they had.
You were a walking trivia card.

People were amazed and often chatted with you,
ended up always arguing with an eight-year-old kid.
I often wondered in amazement how much you knew,
did not know where it came from,
but sports trivia was good for you.

Basketball became your pastime
even though you never played on a team.
But you managed to develop some good techniques.

Your left-handed writing
could hardly be seen.
You needed a magnifying glass
to determine it's context and meaning.

In high school you became the Class Clown,
always in trouble for running the class.
A show you will always put on.
Teachers would tell me, "If only he stopped clowning around."
This is not a comedy club.

Popularity came to you as naturally as your smile.
People loved you because you always managed
to bring them to laughter.
You soon became the "JOSHER,"
a stage name dubbed by your co-workers.

You are now of legal age.
Sometimes it is hard to imagine that you are an adult,
that my little boy is all grown up,
a man and on his own,
having a good life.

Joshinzski was the name I called you as a child when I wanted your attention.
Joshua Pierre when I was angry at you.
My little Joshua when you were good.
I now call you Joshua as a man.

But to me you will always be my Josh, your nickname, because I am proud of you!

Adrian

Born on a windy day in September,
you were tiny in features but cute as a button.
Six pounds, six ounces,
you had sky blue eyes.
Bald like a bald eagle,

you looked like Sweet Pea, Popeye's son.
You would often leave one eye open and the other closed.
Your rosy cheeks and blond hair made you look like a cherub;
your face as a newborn seemed to be angelic.

Everyone wanted to hold you
because you were so easygoing,
hardly cried or fussed.
You were happy all the time,
always smiling, eyes bright and shining.

At one year old, you started talking,
and boy could you talk.
People were amazed
because you were so tiny.

I remember when you were five you got lost
in the biggest flea market in Fort Lauderdale.
All of a sudden, through the loudspeaker
came an announcement—my whole complete name was given,
address, and phone number too! I said, "Wait a minute, that's me they are
asking for!"
Like a little lost sheep, my son Adrian had vanished,
but you were such a smart cookie
that you weren't lost for long, for you gave so much information
you were found right away.

You were such a good student, always getting A's and B's.
Artistic since childhood, you began to draw.
You won art contests, for your imagination was vivid.
I must say you got your creativity from your mom.

Claribel Coreano

In high school you did good.
Although quiet and into football,
you managed to keep good grades.
You won many weightlifting contests
and you strived for the best.

You were interested in fitness
and keeping healthy at best.
High school seemed to have passed by so fast for you.
You were so responsible, working and studying.
Graduation came in no time.

You were a responsible young man,
committed to your job,
signed up for every branch in the military.
You had a tendency to negotiate what you wanted
until you found the right area to go into.

Now at twenty years old and
on your own, living independently,
your goals are within reach
and you will be leaving soon
to serve your country.

I pray that God will watch over you
and keep you safe and healthy
until you come back to us
to share your experiences.

I know that you will accomplish great things
in your life as long as you keep focused.
I remember just two decades ago
I was holding you in my arms and rocking you to sleep.

Andrewinski was the name I called out to get your attention.
Adrian Renee when I was mad at you.
My little "H" when were you were good.
I now call you Adrian as a man.

But to me you will always be my Sweet Pea, your nickname, because
you were so helpful!

JUSTIN

Born on a hot day in the summer,
your hair black and with a
blond streak like a gremlin.
Your cheeks were red and had two beautiful dimples
which made you appear as though
you were always smiling.

You were a big baby with long legs and arms,
healthy and strong,
your skin clear and soft,
chubby cheeks red and rosy.

My third child,
pregnancy was swift, no complications.
Your birth was so smooth, thirty minutes in duration.
Born on a Father's Day,
you were a gift for your dad.

You were a good baby,
always smiling,
an appetite like a bear,
smart and happy
until two years old
when your hyperactivity started to surge.

It was hard to keep track of you,
wanting to do everything the older kids did,
getting into anything and everything,
trying to grow up before your time.

I kept you in check.
Kindergarten came.
You were okay,
did very well,
although asthma hit you
and made you get sick frequently.

Claribel Coreano

You entered Magnet School
at second grade.
Your intelligence was noticeable.
An honor student since then,
you were doing advanced work
and getting good grades.
You were at the same school till eighth grade.

You tried Pop Warner Football for a while
then music became your interest,
first the flute, then the saxophone, trumpet, and then keyboards,
from instrument to writing music, lyrics, and raps.
A karaoke machine is now your pastime.

Freshman year was a tough year for you.
You got confused because your father left.
So sad you became.
It's not your fault, Son, you are great.
It's just that people change….
Don't focus on our mistakes.

It's been hard to keep you focused
because you are only fifteen years old, and tall—almost six feet.
But inside, just a scared teen.
You look older than your age
because of the way you handle yourself,
but I know deep down you are just my little boy.

Justino was the name I called you to make sure you looked at me.
Justin Michael when you got me upset.
My "Just" when you were good.
I now call you Justin as a young teen.

But to me you will always be my Justin Music Box, your nickname
because you make music with everything and anything you find!

Stephen

Born on a cool fall morning in November,
boy you gave me a struggle—two days in labor.
I thought you were never going to arrive,
but when you did, a beautiful child, tranquil spirit,
black, long hair. My reaction when I first saw you
was, "Hey, I have a rock star."
The nurses said, "When he grows up all the ladies
will go crazy at the distinctive birthmark."

What a cute baby you were, a gentle soul,
smiled at everything you saw.
No fuss nor crying at all,
you seemed happy all the time.

I remember when you were one how you
always fell asleep eating in your high chair—
your face was always full of food,
covering your plate. I have pictures that will tell.

Your favorite pastime was putting on your
father's military uniform shirt and
walking around with his boots.
What a thrill that was for you.
It showed how much you admired your father.
You were always the first to greet him at the door.

You played Little League baseball,
hit a home run at five.
What a joy to see you play.
Your hat was bigger than your head
and you hit the ball as hard as you could.
You played good for being such a small kid.

When you started school, you were quiet and shy.
It was hard for the teacher to get a word out of you.
You enjoyed drawing cartoons especially Dragon Ball Z.
I was amazed at how well you drew since the age of three.

Claribel Coreano

You are now almost a teenager.
It's hard to believe how fast time has gone by.
My baby has grown up so quickly, and why?

Teen years are the hardest, and you are my last.
Trial and error—I hope that things go smoothly with you.
To be able to enjoy your years,
Bear in mind that I am getting older.
I know that you will be a good kid,
because you are obedient and respectful.

I hope that life will bring joy and happiness
like the sunshine you have brought me.
You are always happy and are a jokester.

Steven is the name I call you when I want your attention.
Stephen C…. when I am mad at you.
My little Stevie when you are good.
Stephen I call my teenager

But to me you will always be "wee bee," your nickname, because you
will always be my baby!

I Am Me!

Discovery of a new woman
Who has found her inner strength through God,
Spiritually re-awakened to find out that he is the only way,
Enlightened to know that through his love and mercy
Anyone can be saved.

A new woman I've become,
With hope and a future,
To know that through grace Christ has saved my dying soul,
Helped me see a horizon, and uplifted my spirits.
Guide me into the path of wisdom,
Teach me faith and patience,
Provide me with assurance by means of prayers.

I have reached a new insight in my life,
That my joy comes from God.
He has taught me to love others,
To reach out and bring forth hope in others,
Let them know that he is the only way,
That this world is empty without him.

The life that I was living was not the one he set out for me.
I was wasting my days and years on worldly things,
confused and suffering because of sins.
I realized that what I needed:
Needed his refuge,
Needed his guidance,
Needed his unconditionally love.
What he gave me in return was his forgiveness.
Blessed me with salvation.
Blessed me with understanding.
Blessed me with wisdom.
Gave me hope in my life.
I thank you, Lord, for your love and sacrifice.

What Has Become of "ME"?

I am not the same old woman I used to be.
I think so differently; can you catch a glimpse of me?
I was young, naïve, and innocent; I saw life in another way.
I did not know how to defend myself.
My self-esteem was too low.
I had been asked, how did you let it last so long?
Don't ask me; I don't know.
Only if you had been there and done that
Could you relate.
The important thing that matters is that I broke away.
Imagine if I would have stayed.
My life would have been in the palm of his hand.
For as years go by, the pain gets stronger
And the punishment by the hands of a man
Gets rougher and more repetitive.
So thank God that I found an open door.
A little window was left open for me to breathe some fresh air.
And know that I can go out.
Stretch away in a small space like Alice in Wonderland,
I find myself as a small person in a giant space,
Closed in a glass house too fragile to break through.
Everything around me was slowly falling apart
By the sound of his scream that was like thunder.
His curses could make a deaf ear burst in fear.
His malicious intentions were planned so well
And his future he set away.
This is the life of a wife beater.
This is the story of a survivor.
His story is easy to detail. I know how manipulating he is in his way.
Things come easy for him,
But I've just begun to live again.
For I was trapped in a glass house with no exit to be found.
I became stronger and made everything
smash to smithereens with hope
Until I was free to be myself again....
This is the story of a survivor.
"I am alive and well."

Alone

Just the other day I was thinking of how my life has
just passed me by and left me all alone
My family is far away and their lives are separate from mine
Days are going by so fast and everyone is growing up
They are getting married, becoming teenagers, and growing old
And here I am alone

The friends I thought were my friends no longer could be found
The man I thought would be with me forever left long ago with someone
else
My children are almost all gone and I will be left all alone

I always wanted to grow old together with my companion
Do all the things I dreamed off when I was younger
Do things I did not get a chance to do because I was a busy mother
Accomplish all my goals and dreams till I run out of ideas
But I have not found my partner, friend, and lover
And time is running out

Once you hit forty, men act like you are damaged goods
They see no future; half of your life has been spent
They evaluate you by the decades instead
The heart doesn't matter anymore, oh no, not these days
What they look for is a sexy body to model
And a trophy to display
What a pity—it's their loss not mine
Here I am alone and happy to love me

For if you can stand yourself enough to love being on your own
What more can you want from a man
If no one is here to scream, or shout, or look down on me,
Or call me names, to mock me, or control?
I thank God that I was saved from continuing my life
In a living hell with a selfish man
Yes, I am all alone but there is only one being on
Heaven or earth I won't be without—that is my God,
My savior and company that has never left my side
Now he is a reliable being that no one should be without

17

Fragile Rose

A good woman is like a fragile rose
You have to treat her with tender love and care
Like a rose, she is special
In gentleness, you need to handle her with attention

So that her petals don't fly off
You have to nourish the rose with water
Take care of her each day
For if one day you don't care for her
you will see her slowly die away

A good woman is like a precious crystal
Thin, clear, and shining
That you can see right through
You need to handle with special consideration
So that she doesn't fall and shatter
Like the finest crystal
You need to keep her high on a pedestal of respect
Handle her with caution each day
Crystal is so fragile that when it falls it disintegrates
Into bits and pieces so fine
You cannot find each piece
And will never put the crystal back the same way
Pieces will still be missing

A good woman is like a shining diamond in the rough
Of the best value in all the world
Only a master jeweler can see her value and appreciate who she is
Hold her delicately like a precious jewel of the Nile
To shine bright and let her light illuminate the skies
Display her like an expensive jewel so others know that she is yours
Don't hide her away in a jewelry box
She will lose her luster and sparkle
Show her off so others can see how beautiful
and how kind she is to you

A woman is like buried treasure
Every day you can find some new jewels inside her heart
Her charming ways
Her loving heart
Her kindness
Are all gems that are very hard to find
Value her when you have her
Cherish her for all she is
Love her with your heart, soul, and mind
And she will always give back the equivalent to you

Don't misplace or lose her
Because a good woman is hard to find
You might search and search all your life
And never find the same jewel you had in your hands
The one which you allowed to slip away
In your mind you will always be thinking
If only I would have kept her,
If only I would have taken care of her
If only I would have valued her
If only I would have respected her
If only I would have loved her enough
If only I would have given myself in mind, heart, and soul
What-**ifs**……..
Are only regrets
What-**ifs** don't change anything
Don't wait until it is too late for you to find her
Because as fragile, valuable, and beautiful as a woman is …
Once she makes up her mind and decides
There is no turning back
Nothing and no one will convince her otherwise
Grasp her now while there is still a moment in time
To mend her broken heart
And show her that you care
Hurry up and don't waste anymore time
Time is passing by fast
The hours, minutes, seconds, days, months, years are going by so fast
There is still time if you want to seize the day
And finally make her yours
Love her until death

You will not have any regrets….
A beautiful jewel, rose, and crystal is yours to value, hold,
and keep till you both grow old

Lessons Learned From My Mistakes ...

This is for every young woman who is not sure what to do
or what choices to make.
Remember that in life many opportunities will come your way.

First, make education your priority, for
it is the ticket for self-independence.
Remember an education represents respect, integrity,
the ability to afford things you would not be able to otherwise.

Save yourself for your soul mate, don't abuse your temple,
be very careful not to fall into temptation,
do not allow others to abuse your body.
Always remember that there are selfish individuals out there
who would like to take with no intentions of staying or respecting you
afterwards.

It is more special to wait for that special individual
who would share his life with you,
who will become your partner in life,
appreciate your sacrifice, and always stay by your side.

Choose your friends wisely, guard your reputation with dignity
so others can see that they have to respect you.
Don't be afraid to say no, I am not ready yet.
Listen to the wisdom of the elders—they've been there,
done that, and know what it is to fail.

For I have learned a lot from my mistakes.
I have suffered greatly for my errors.
In life you get one chance only to do things right.
If you mess up, life gets very hard after that.
Things become complicated,
individuals look down on you,
people you trust leave you,
husbands abandoned you,
nor will men want you or respect you.
I encourage you to do things right the first time.
Don't let anything get in your way,

21

not even the harsh words of others who try to keep your spirit down.
Remember that they will always be waiting for you to fail, so do not give them
The Win ...

I Know What I Want

I know now more than ever what I really want out of life. I am also very certain of all the things I want in a man.

I know what I want and I know what I deserve. I will not settle for less. Even if it means waiting to meet my soul mate in my later years, I will wait patiently for my partner, friend, confidant, and soul mate to arrive

No need to rush into any relationship, for what if I don't feel it's right? For in my heart I know what I really want. I am not looking for perfection, not great looks or money.

I am just waiting for the individual who can be my other half, who will respect, love, and cherish me in every way, accept all my imperfections and say, "Honey, its okay."

For real love is meaningful, understanding, and accepting. It is not just about intimacy; it's more about loving unconditionally the person for who they are.

What good is it if a person is beautiful on the outside and shallow inside?

What good is it if a person has all this money and feels this is all they can offer?

What good is it if a person feels he is great in bed but does not respect you afterwards?

What good is it if he gives everything he can give but, on the other hand, makes you feel misery in all the things he says?

What good is it if a person has a great job and education but cannot communicate with the most important person in his life?

What good is it if a person has the greatest personality around his friends but is cruel and vain with his family?

What good is it if a person is successful in every way but lacks the most important skill of all—empathy for others?

What good is it if a person has self-esteem but gained it by belittling others by refusing to accept all his insecurities and says, "I am okay but you are not"?

What good is it if an individual is narcissistic and has a grandiose idea that they can only be understood by anyone who is considered special or of high status?

What good is it if an individual is arrogant and conceited, who interpersonally exploits others to achieve his needs?

What good is it if an individual says he based himself on truth but then does not practice it?

I am waiting for an individual who is searching for the truth and not one who thinks he is the "TRUTH"; so far there is not one perfect being in this world but God! And that is my "truth."

The truth is in the asking. How else would you know the truth? I want somebody who is honest, caring, warm, family oriented, committed to me, who loves diversity, cultural differences, is funny, witty, silly, and not afraid to express his feelings so I can know when to be supportive and not wonder is he okay? I know what I want and I will wait to get it. I am not going to settle for less because I know I deserve it.

A Woman of Substance

A woman of substance knows what she wants and what she is worth
She knows that in life you must sacrifice
She understands that sometimes
She must separate herself to give others their space
She believes in miracles, she believes in love
She believes in saving herself for a worthy individual

A woman of substance has faith in things to come
And if she is rejected she accepts that there are better things in line
She has hope in her future and has faith for a better life
She sees the beauty in everyone she meets
She shares of herself without any qualms

A woman of substance believes in the things she cannot see
Trusts that she must let God be the guide of her life
Thrives to become close to God, let others know of the miracle in her life
A woman of substance is responsible to society
Must work and study towards self-independence
Is secure enough to share her wealth and wisdom with her partner

Her trust is in the Lord, and those who meet her will know
That her light shines bright and is not hard to find
For she is guided by the Holy Spirit and tries to live her life in peace
She shares her love with those around her
Takes time to share with her loved ones
Takes care of her family and children
Still has time for her other half
A woman of substance displays God's love all around her

What better choice than to love a woman who demonstrates her love for
God?
You will be confident that she will always be by your side
With no doubts or any fear you can share your life with her
For a woman of substance is hard to find....
Don't lose this one! Is this your last chance?

Throughout Your Lifetime

*Throughout your lifetime you get the chance to make decisions in life
that will affect your present and your future.
Either you choose to make the right choices or
you lose focus on other things and make the wrong decisions.
I was at one point a beautiful, young, and virile woman
who had everything going for her,
but because of stupidity I ended up wasting my life
on individuals who never gave anything back to me.
I learned the hard way and faced many consequences
as a result of my bad choices.
I struggled for years to raise and care for my children;
for years now this has been my lot in life and is still going on.
Yes, it's responsibility, and I have accepted my fate in life.
I know who I am! I know what I want!
I understand that I could have done things differently,
but why dwell on the past? It's not going to bring anything back!
I don't live a dream because I know that not all dreams come true;
I don't live in a fantasy because I know that it will not be realistic!
But I do have goals, and I plan for them and strive to achieve them.
I measure my resources, define what is needed,
and if by chance I fail ... then I can always try again.
The only difference is that those individuals that failed will eventually
give up.
I do acknowledge that I get discouraged,
but I keep trying in faith and with hope for a better future.
Believe me, my ego is not self-absorbed,
I know that it is okay to think big and dream,
because you never know when God's eyes will find grace upon me
and with his mercy bless me just the same.*

*I know that I don't have a Master's or Doctorate, but life training has
given me
all the schooling and wisdom that I need for now.
And what greater intelligence is there than the wisdom life has to spare
and the humble spirit the Lord shares with those who endure life's
adversities?
I am an individual who knows who she is, who knows what she wants,
who knows her own flaws, knows her own*

limits, and knows what I can offer someone else.
I am not rich but rich in love for the children that
God has given me, are treasures from beyond.
I am simple in my ways; no need to pretend to be someone else's high
in a dream but crashing into self-destruction at the end.
I can't wear the mask the other individuals want me to wear,
because I am me, and I am happy being me.
I do not need to impress anyone in order to be accepted or wanted.
I have always been this way and will never change.
I do, however, love people, have sympathy,
and I empathize with others whose plight in life is of suffering.
I am not sure why.
But God has always used me in helping others,
and as I can remember as a child I always stated that I wanted to help
others in need.
I ask God if it is his will and if it is in his plan for me to do so.
You see, he has a plan for everyone and a mission in life,
but at times we tend not to listen to his call and do whatever we want.
I am very open-minded; I am fair, caring, and warm.
Why search anywhere else when you've got it all right here?
Throughout our lifetime the decisions we make
can determine our present and future if we are quick and wise to make ...
or choose ... the right individual, partner, lover, or soul mate
Who will be my once in a lifetime?
I am wishing that it could be you ...

Reflections

I have reached a point in my life
where I, as a woman, know how much I value me.
I matured as years went by,
realized that I am comfortable with myself
being alone without any fears or concerns.
Comfortable with my presence,
not to say that I do not enjoy good companionship,
I love people and love to share with others
but I am happy spending time on my own.
In my aloneness I dedicate my time
to painting and writing hobbies not that well developed,
but I enjoy just the same.

Creative being that I am, I love diversity of all kinds,
even in the food I cook and eat.
Emeril's bang, "Beware of me."

I love to help others grow and share my hope instead of blight.
Soon enough they too will see that in faith hope can grow.
My Spirit cries to the Lord each day; I pray and pray.
God's silence is not denial; he answers quietly all my prayers.
Soon the miracle I await will one day come true in faith.

My soul cries out, "Lord let me be a vessel of peace
instead of anger I negate."
I want to be known not for I what I possess nor give
but for what I have become spiritually.
Material things don't matter.
Greed and money are not my obsession.
Simple ways that are everlastingly me.
No need to impress me. I am too hard to amuse.
I don't believe in superficiality.

Hypocrisy I can see a mile away, it does not fool me, not a bit,
Don't even try it!
I like a straight, honest answer.
"Shoot as the crow flies!"
Don't beat around the bush; be clear and say what you mean,

As long as it is the truth.
Remember, the truth can set you free....
I don't try to impress others; if they don't like me that's their option.
As long as I am happy with me, I know that God loves me all the same.

Walk your talk, talk your walk.
Do not deceive with lies and scorns.
Soon everything will come to light.
Reality hits and you will be a fool in disguise.
Emancipate your negative view.
Be positive in all your do.

Love does not come easy it has been said
But don't ignore when it's in front of your face.
Next time it will be hard to catch a glimpse.
Difficult is just a word for the coward.
Take risks—not everything is planned in an organizer.
Live life with some spontaneity; do plan, but expect diversity.
Learn to live for today and tomorrow.
The future no one knows.
The past is already gone.
So why fret on what I could have done or said,
What I could have accomplished or gained?
Nothing stays for very long,
Not even the color of my hair.
Soon it will be gray and thin.
Signs of aging will not fade.
Wisdom I will have gained.
Mature woman enough to say
what I feel in my heart to say,
what I think I should say.
What I hope to say
what I want others to hear.
Nothing will quiet this strong, assertive woman anymore.
I reach a momentum in life scores.
Love my children, love my life,
love my God.
Thanks to him, I see another view of life.
I am who I am—no need to change.
What I have become is special in all ways.

The strength and growth are here to stay.
I am no longer ever afraid.
Stay clear of me.
I am self-made, a new creation of God in its place.

I Remember the Early Years of My Life ...

I

I remember when I was three years old,
in a white rocking chair I fell asleep with my raggedy doll.
I was wearing a pink cotton dress with flowers sewn up on the front.
I never understood the reason why I was left;
all I know is that I had a new stepmom and a new grandma.

I remember that I relied on my imagination
to keep me company when no one was around
and I often fantasized about the silhouette of my mom.
I don't remember a hug nor receiving any love from my new family.
All I remember is that I was left to fend for myself.
I was taken everywhere alone with a chauffer.
I traveled to many places, went to the finest restaurants,
went to the best beaches, but was alone inside my heart.

I remember playing with the sand, building castles with a bucket and a shovel.
I collected sea shells and tropical fishes.
I would always put them on display in empty soda bottles.
I drank sea water like it was juice and ate sea grapes till I turned green.
I was an explorer and a good one, I must say,
for I was always dissecting everything that came my way.

I remember how much I loved chasing butterflies.
I whispered softly, "Ven mi mariposa, ven," (Come, my butterflies, come my way),
and then on my shoulder a butterfly would softly lie.
My body in still motion, I would caress my newfound friend,
for nature was my only friend.
I collected lizards, slugs, and beetles.
I would name them exclusively with silly names.
I had ducks, I had goats, and I had a parrot to talk to at all times.

During the summer I would camp out in the old mansion
that was previously owned by a dictator,
which appeared more like a haunted mansion.
There were many almond trees at which
I fancied throwing rocks until
I knocked enough almonds for me to eat.
I remember how the hibiscus was my candy flower;
whenever I got hungry this was what I reached for.

I made bonfires at night and counted stars all night long.
I was fascinated by space and how everything came together.
At times, difficult questions came to mind but I was too young to
analyze.
Therefore, I thought it was often silly to think the way I thought.

II

Days of rain were my favorite, especially the days when the rains
came down like buckets, and I would stand next to the water spout
as if a shower head was installed. I stood there free floating in water
until my lips were purple and my skin shriveled in the cold water.
Memorable moments which I wish would have never ended,
for during those years I don't remember pain,
for I was in touch with nature and loved life too well,
did not know any fears or dangers as well.
I can now think of the innocence I felt.

Some days during the evenings I would camp out in the backyard,
use wood for fire, and cook for myself.
My creativity was at an all-time high. I made rock people to play,
made furniture from small match boxes and cans.
I made my own town of dirt, rocks, and leaves,
for the best toys are nature made.

When back at home, I would again sit in my white rocking chair,
rocking my raggedy doll, pretending to read the newspaper at age three,
until to my own shock I began reading at four and my stepmom, in
shock,
Thought I was a genius and put me into public school during the day,
private in the afternoon.

School was fun, but only due to recess,
for there were so many kids bigger than me in class.
I was still a small child, didn't care much for work.
All I wanted was to play
and be free like yesterday.
I remember learning how to count with an abacus.
It was the most amazing thing for me
even though math never came easily.

As I grew older I matured, and
by the age of eight I finally felt what
my heart had been feeling since age three.
I was such a child in pain
but had no clue how, when, and why I got there.
I missed my parents and my days began to get cloudy,
for now I knew how long it had been since I last saw my parents.
Sadness began to creep into me and I did not have anyone
to listen to my worries.

I often cried myself to sleep at night,
Wishing and hoping to meet my parents.
Nature and everything around me began to look dark and grey.
I found myself alone in space
until the day I met my parents.

Life Realities

Childhood Dreams

Childhood dreams are of cotton candy, pink bubble gum,
and peppermint candies
In the land of childhood dreams where anything goes ...
Dreams of clouds form funny characters in the skies
The sun shines bright
I stare and stare into nowhere
It looks like a big orange in the sky
The sun follows me everywhere I go
I see my shadow in the road as I walk
If you look at the sun for a very long time,
you begin to see many spots before your eyes

The moon looks like cheese
as it smiles back at me
A big bulb in the sky
Illuminating the night in the heavens
In the middle of the night I see a star
I wish upon the stars
that all my dreams can come true,
that I get to meet one day my childhood prince
or my knight and shining armor
like in the fairy-tale books

I see the flowers amongst the fields,
a spread of pretty colors,
of daisy, lilies, roses, and wild flowers
springing through the air a sweet and gentle fragrance
A swarm of bees flies by
They come to rest in their homeland

Along the path I see a road leading to a beautiful, colorful rainbow
A pot of gold is at the end of the rainbow—it's a fable
I catch a glimpse of
fairies flying all around the enchanted forest
beaming lights as I walk by,
guiding me towards the light

Many elves protect the forest
and warn others of my trouble in my journey
to welcome me into my sweet childhood dreams
of childhood-innocence reflections
Wishes, dreams, and hopes make up a sweet childhood dream
We all at one point or another view life in the same fantasy

This Is Your Life

Does it matter how you have lived it?
Does it make a difference what you gain?
Will it matter if you forfeited it for fortune or for fame?
Does it even make zilch of a difference if you use others in vain?
Are you really happy with yourself or accept the things you could have changed?

Or do you just go on living the days for what they are—*"existence"*?
Routine has become your area of expertise.
Perfection is what you seek, even in the toothpaste you brush your teeth with!
Let me see what I have included in my "to-do list."
I plan my day so well; I have to feel pleasure every day.
Nothing matters if I am not instantly gratified,
And darned if my needs are not met.
Sacrificing is a word I do not know exists!
Can I ask you, "What have you given of yourself today?"
Have you really done something that matters? Or are you just living for yourself?

Keep on living in a lie! Denying the things you must heed to change,
Denying the past that enslaves you,
Denying the life that God has designed for you,
Denying the light inside your heart that is trying to break free and finally come out.
Live to tell a thousand lies.
You even think that time will stop for you this time,
Keep you young and adolescent. What a shame that you can't even accept maturity as well.

Does it matter that in your selfishness you hurt, use, and discard people
In the same way you wear different underwear—something so personal, really?
But you are so indiscreetly manipulative and misleading in your ways.
The truth will set you free, don't you think?
If you accept the truth then you don't have to feel so guilty!

What kind of life do you live,
Thinking God does not see everything,
That every lie, deception, and sin will not come to light one day?
Why hide? Why pretend? Why try to be something you are not? Why
live somebody else's life? What do you get out of it? Don't you feel
empty and vain?

I feel so saddened by your pride.
I am sorry about your arrogance.
My heart breaks because of your lies.
I am concerned about your selfishness.
You think that your pedestal is too high for me to reach.
What a mistake, I must say,
To think that I don't match to your potential.
You feel superior and think that you are better than me
Just because you think that you are so intellectual.
How sad to think that you measure your surroundings by a caste system
instead.
Please get down from the pedestal.
Come down to earth—it's time to face the truth!

God doesn't rejoice with the conceited,
But the humble he brings forward.
As if! You made a pact with the devil to gain fame, money, and attention,
Hoping to become rich in a moment of desperation.
For what? To spend it all in a day, month, or year?
Will you spend all of it just on yourself for on one else matters?
Money is the root of all evil. When you have it you desire to gain more.
To share? Not really! Just for me—"I" only exist.
The things that we desire the most are sometimes not beneficial.
Most often you will lose your soul instead of losing your pride.
You will get deeper in your desires and indulgence
And see that nothing you do matters because you can buy your way out.

Look in the mirror of life;
Scrutinize the weak areas as if you're looking deeply at a map.
Seek out the harmful things and expel them out.
Have will power, seek out good judgment,
Experience self-control, and don't overindulge in pleasures.
Stop it already—God did not make you an addict

Nor were you born with a tag that states, "He will be an addict for the rest of his life."
You have no excuse! You can stop it if you want!
Don't sell your soul to the devil
Just so you can experience pleasure.

Remember that God made you from his imagine and your body is his temple.
You will have to meet him face to face one day.
Face judgment, and what would you say?
God, the life you gave me has made me this way?
No excuse would you have that day!
No time will you have to hide!
No time to either negotiate or manipulate!
What would you say when God asks,
"How did you spend your life?"
Remember that he will show you your life
Just like scenes from the movies.
No scenes will be cut out, no retakes or mistakes.
Your life will be live and uncut.
Everything will come out that day.
God will say, *"This is your Life."*
No forgiveness will be given,
For that will be the last day of the rest of your life.

Live for Today

Live for today, for who knows what tomorrow may bring
Do today what you can do at the moment; don't delay
Tomorrow will be yet another day
Be happy, for this is the day the Lord has made
Bring about your best in spite of any feelings of gloom
Smile bright; let your teeth shine
Give your love to all as if it is the last day of your life

Live for today, for who knows what will happen in the future
Just remember that the future no one knows
It's puzzling even for those who think they do
They understand it's never clear
The design plan cannot be forfeited or manipulated
The hands of God control everything
I wouldn't challenge him

Live for today, for who knows what tomorrow may bring
Disaster strikes and it does not make an appointment
Accidents happen; they don't pre-warn us
Tragedy occurs, doesn't leave you a note beforehand
If Death knocks on your door
What will you say? "Hey hold on, I have too much to accomplish.
Please go away—come back another day"?
Will Death look you in the eye
and say, "Yeah sure, whenever you are ready"?

Don't indulge in unhealthy habits
Like unprotected sex in the heat of the moment
By seeking pleasure you could become the walking dead
Become infected with a slow death
Drinking itself can put you in harm's way
Inhibitions are the lowest, and if you drive
It's like playing Russian roulette
Don't smoke, watch your diet,
and in everything you do, do it in moderation
Everything in excess is a sin
Prevention is the key to helping you see another tomorrow
Remember that you never know when this day
Will be the last day of your life

What Can I Do to Change What Has Happened?

THE PAST

What can I do to change the past? For there is no train to take you back
No token given, no free passes, nor a free ride back to the last track
The past is the last stop, and a dead end awaits
The past is gone, no need to bring it back
What can change if you go back?
Would you be able to think and say I will not make the same mistake again?
Are you sure that can be done? For no one gets a second chance to go
What's done is done!
What's finished is finished!
No need to try to fix the mess you left; no way you can clean it
Don't cry over spilled milk; that's what's been said
It's been spoiled, a long time ago
So what's the use of thinking about the past?

Let it go, set it free, live and let live
Forget the past, erase the memories
No thinking back, please!
Don't let the ghosts of memories past haunt you
For they can create an illusion of self-defeat
They make you think you have been cheated
It makes you feel so guilty
No need to let it haunt you; send it away
Think of a blank slate
The past is just a white page in my book
The present is what I will write about

PRESENT

The present is yours to make it transpire
A gift from God, that is what it is
Learn to live one day at a time
Learn to give what you don't possess
Love till you can no longer give of yourself
For love makes many miracles happen
If ever you doubt that it can come about

Just look up to the sky
Admire the beauty
Look towards the ocean
And the waves softly caressing the sea

PRESENT

That is truly amazing!
The present is me in action
Making every effort to make it happen
I will make my dreams come true
God is there to see me through
I know that if I stay true to myself
I will find the way to make it real
For I have learned from past mistakes
But I am not willing to look back
I am determined to live in the present
I love my life no matter what
No trials or tribulations will keep my hopes down
I will look towards the horizon and see a rainbow in the sky
My trust is in the Lord, for his words tell me not to worry
For he knew me even before I was to be born
My life has been known to him; the plans he has
I am just discovering
The present is a gift for you to have

FUTURE

The future no one knows about
So don't worry about things to come
Don't try to predict what you will have
No one knows if you will be dead or alive
The future holds many secrets
Like a Pandora's box it shines with crystals, gems, and diamonds
It pulls you in and temptation overpowers you
Don't look in, don't open the box
Don't touch it, it is not yet time
The future is not to be known by anyone
For God changes plans and often directions
Don't try to precipitate what's going to happen
You think that what you see is what you are going to get
No way! For the future holds many surprises
I would not mess with the future

43

God knows the beginning and the end
God is in control; he will do it his way
He will open the doors and bless your life in the future
For he knows what's right for you and me
He knows the timing, he knows what it takes
I do not want to get out of God's timing, I want to trust in his timing
And let him show me the way
He knows what needs to happen before the future is set

How Do You Define Happiness?

How do you define happiness? To everyone it varies in
meaning:
For some it is money, wealth, fame, fortune, women, men, and drugs.

But are they really happy or content with money?
Money is their main obsession.
The goal becomes to make more and more
Until the worries of losing it take over,
The fear that others will attempt to steal it,
The disappointment when losing some,
The anger when they don't want to pay up.
That sounds like too much anxiety,
So I do not think money brings happiness.

To be born into a **wealthy** family,
That does not bring happiness.
Imagine how it will feel to carry a title
That often is not even yours?
It's been thrown over from generation to generation,
And to some they think this is what makes them a unique person,
To say I can get away with doing harm,
For I belong to "such and such," I have a privilege.
I can get out of every scam;
My title will outsmart them all.
Spoiled characters and selfish pride,
That's what a title brings with it at times.

Whoever said that **fame** can bring you happiness?
Fame is just a shadow of superficiality
That let's people live two lives,
One in front of others and the other behind closed doors.
Famous people are put on a pedestal so high
That when people realize that they have failed
They go into shock.
For how is it that an individual who is supposed to be flawless
Gets into drugs, drinks all their problems away, or takes their own life?
It's obvious fame and fortune do not make you happy

When you have a **fortune** and invest in it more and more.
You own practically the whole monopoly
But ignore those who are hungry and poor,
Invest to destroy the ecosystem by building more malls,
Big tall buildings that reach the sky,
Amazing office spaces that make less space for schools.
Housing is lacking for many
But to you there is no clue.
You ignore the plight of others
As long as you can accumulate riches.
Fortune is your bliss.
Your arrogance keeps people at bay.
Happiness is far away from your fortune cookies today!

For those who think that having many relationships,
Whether a **man or woman,** is going to bring happiness,
Then no clue have you about the meaning of life.
You search and search for something
That is missing inside of your heart,
A piece that has been taken by
The plight of losing a mom or a dad
Or not having their love at one point or another.
To search to fill the void and emptiness
That no one has been able to fulfill,
You think if someone can love you stronger
You will finally reach happiness.
But what a mistake!
Happiness comes from the inside out.
Love yourself first and then seek to love someone else.
No one can make you happy or bring you happiness.
Only you hold the key to your own contentment.

Drugs are a temporary feeling.
They numb the pain of life and trick your mind into
Thinking you're happy for a very short time.
After it's all over, downwards you fall.
No longer "happy," you go for it again.
Happiness is not an instant feeling
Nor a temporary joy.
Happiness lasts and lasts all day long, months and months,
Years and years …

Have you happened to stop
And think that you could find happiness
in the very simple things of life?
For happiness could be many beautiful things
That many do close the eyes to.
Let me set the case in point by saying that
It is a joy you feel that
no matter how difficult your problems may be
You feel joy no matter what.

A joy from watching the stars.
A joy from just being alive.
A joy to know that God is in charge.
It is as simple as............
The first cry of a newborn baby
Or the sound of the birds singing early in the morning
Or the sound of waves in the ocean
Or just watching the sunset at sundown;

Just watching your child grow from a child into a man,
The warmth and care of a stranger who thanks you
For all you have done for them,
The simplicity in life treasures,
Those things you cannot ignore.
Joy can come about from admiring nature at its finest.
Walking in a forest, admiring the trees,
Exploring the seashores for fish,
Respecting nature for all it gives,
Being the best you can be,
Loving God first and then others,
That is truly true joy.
Helping a fellow man during a tribulation,
Taking time for your family,
Taking time for yourself,
Taking time to be grateful,
Taking time to thank God for the joy
He has given you, for that is the only true joy;
That no matter what you lack,
financially, materially, or in status,

In his presence we are everything.
For we are princes and princesses
And our father is a King of Heaven.

The Best Way To Be Rich

Everyone looks for a way to get rich
But is there really such a thing as being rich?
Does having so much really make you complete?
Some individuals who are rich are still running on empty
Nothing satisfies the emptiness in their heart
Seek and seek
And they don't find
Buy and buy
And nothing ever satisfies
Invest and invest
And it never seems to be enough money
But do pleasure and more pleasure really make you happy? Thinking you
are indispensable and that everything is purchasable?
Think about it: does it mean you are really rich?
Or is there something missing? The spirit knows what it needs to be rich
The spirit yearns to grow and be free
The spirit knows that a person who gives of him/herself
Is far richer than any monetary figure on Wall Street
For what the spirit seeks, nothing in this earth can satisfy
Look to heaven where a greater spirit dwells
For we are made in his image
And seek the spiritual plane

Some individuals are rich in love
The life they live is for nurturing others; they give love,
Show love, and are a living proof of love

Some individuals are rich by the way they reach out to others
They give of themselves without waiting for anything back
They help others gain insight on life
They motivate
They encourage
And they believe in God

For they have found the answer to being and feeling really rich
For if you are able to love, forgive, and give of yourself
Then to God you are the richest person on earth

Reality

Reality in life is appalling when you finally accept the truth, which is so painful.
When you finally see what is really in front of your eyes, it is blinding.

Reality in life is shocking; we give and give, never receiving,
Leaving you dull and numb with pain.

Reality in life is outrageous when you decide that this is it; no more games and still your mind debates.

Reality in life is awful when it hits you like a slap in the face and you finally admit it's true, no more haste.

Reality in life is dreadful when you finally say good-bye to an old friend for whom you cared for so long. And this friend doesn't even acknowledge your pain, and faith is battling the cruelty of his rejection.

Reality in life is scandalous when you accept the fact that maybe this friend never has known or will ever know what it is to love.

Reality in life is alarming when you realize that you have been in love with such a lost soul.

Reality in life is unpardonable when you can accept that this is the end and there is no point of no return because pride has gotten in the way. It's sad when you realize that there is no apology nor any remorse; it's scary to know that this is the same person whom you loved all along.

Reality in life is wicked when it hits you like a punch in the face, leaves you in tears and with a heart broken with no remedy to mend it. When your heart aches with the pain of a lover's betrayal, no words are soothing enough to erase the grief.

Reality in life is disgusting when you realize that you were being used like a toy in a toy box: "I got tired of you. I want something new."

Reality is unforgivable when the doll is a human and you forget emotions and feelings you have misled.

Reality in life is honorable when he gets to experience the same pain he caused and be taken for granted in the very same way.

Reality will be my savior when I see that what he has done to me will be done to him.

Times of Turmoil

<u>This is the Story of a Lonely Woman</u>

This is the story of a lonely woman who loved with all her heart
Forgotten and alone,
There in silence she lived and learned
For being a woman is not easy
You could easily fall into the hands of the wrong man
I lived the past of hurt and pain
Shameful, demeaning words my ears heard
No kind words from him
He was just a lesson to be learned
Not to fall into the wrong hands

I struggled for peace
I struggled for freedom
I struggled to be me
I finally set myself free
Of a bondage with no chains,
Of slavery with no master,
But the man who was my husband
I still felt afraid of
A fear I could not ignore

The screaming and the shouting all did not make sense
The pushing and the shoving just to get his way
The anger and controlling was just an escape
His ways were confusing
I never saw right in his words

The days he hit were like a constant nightmare
Did he not know the hows and whys?
Did I deserve such punishment?
Secrets were all over the house
Voices heard that told the truth
Like a whisper in my ear
Live two lives, one during day and one in the night
The secrets soon came out

The light was bright
The cry was heard all over town
For it was the ticket to my freedom
The release of a prisoner
The shackles were broken
The hope came about

The lies that were told,
The truth put them to shame
No remorse in his part
Nor respect in his heart
Just go and be in your way, I said

This is the Story of a Lonely Woman
Who learned life lessons well
I learned that in life you cannot trust a man
A man who hurts you is a coward
A man who cheats is weak
A man who lies is a hypocrite
A man who scorns has a pea-sized self-esteem
A man who lives thinking he is better than anyone else
Is just a confused individual without a soul
So maybe you can get the picture
And see where I am coming from
I am just a lonely woman who managed to break away
From a life ruined by the hands of her man

But that was yesterday; today is now
I learn to live one day at a time
To know how valuable I really am
Not to take crap from any man
I learned my lesson well
I should never be the same

I changed for the better
I lived to tell
I managed to grow
And become whole
I gained all my strength
I gained my dreams
This lonely woman who was lost in fear

Is now the bravest soul
Tell the truth every chance I get
Don't live no lie nor disrespect
I learned that being free
Is the expression to be able to be me

Who steals my heart will know
That I am a good woman with a good soul
Who knows what she is worth
Who knows what she wants
Who knows that in life the most important thing is
To love with all your heart and soul
To have God in your heart
To have respect for others
To forgive and forget
To spread love everywhere you go
And everything that was missing
Comes back to you in the form of a smile
Whether from young or the old
You will feel loved

Sometimes I Feel Angry

I

Sometimes I feel as though God did not see the abuse I went through.
I get angry and upset because my perpetrator is doing so well.
He doesn't suffer financially; he has the world at his feet.
He has a new family as if nothing ever happened.
He has given everything to this woman that he never gave to me
Who had carried the title of his wife for a time.
I see it didn't mean much; it's just a title giving someone possession to
another.
What has happened in my life and the experience I had with this man,
I do not wish it upon anyone; this man had me questioning my own
sanity

Due to the degree of the mind games and manipulation.
My thinking was so thwarted by his accusations, curses, and lack of
remorse
That I began to feel as if I was always at fault.
For how can you explain to someone the actions of an abuser?
How do you describe the cruelty of mind games?
How do you put in simple terms the curses and the verbal abuse?
How can you show the world that inside my home was just a living hell?

How can you try to make others understand that when he talked
He often barked so loud that I would lock my senses out?
How can you show the bruises when they are hidden in your body?
Can you explain PTSD to anybody?
Still, at times I shake when frightened by someone who speaks loud,
Often reliving the scars that are not to be found.

The physical pain goes away with time
But the emotional scars stay forever in your heart.
Bits and pieces will creep up from time to time.
How can I tell the world I was abused by this man?
Hard to believe this man would do such,
For he acts so together; it does not give the impression of being so.

He talks the talk, he portrays the lies,
He hides what he has done so well that no tracks can be uncovered.
His personality of Dr. Jekyll and Mr. Hide,
He let it out only with me and he could not control it.
For I was a woman who tried to fight so hard to stay alive.
He crushed my dreams, he crushed my goals
He made me believe no one would love me at all,
For his control was so effective.

II

I somehow believed that he was so powerful, still
He manipulated my life, he manipulated my children.
He used so many tactics to keep us under his possession.
The threats, the lies, always saying, "Money talks bullshit walks."
He felt untouched by the law; his game they never caught,
For he had connections in every corner with those who would vouch for him.
And like he always said, "One hand washes the other."
For his friends knew of his philandering; he was their hero "man,"
For they all wished they could be like him.
Little did they know of the monster that I knew,
That "Mr. Personality" was just an act that should have won him an Oscar.
I pity those individuals who in the course of these happenings
Were also helping him to do wrong.
For how could you live with yourself knowing that
This man abused his wife and family with no dismay?
I pray for forgiveness every day; that I can forgive those individuals,
Because it's been hard knowing that many caught a glimpse of what happened.
Some witnessed his sins and did nothing.
Others just listened to this man brag of how he kicked his wife around,
Cheated, and lived to tell and joke about it.
Dishonor, scorn, and humiliation: that was what he did to me.
But I know that God was watching and he tried to tell me many times,
"Go, be set free. Leave; it's okay with me."
But due to fear I stayed, thinking it was the right thing to do
And that somehow he would change.
My commitment to my marriage constrained me to stay for so long.

What a mistake! I now know that God would have wanted me to leave
A very long time ago, you see…. I am sorry, God. I was to blind to see
The open door that he was showing me and I kept on living a lie
As an alternative to living in reality.
Life was not intended to be spent like that;
God does not want any woman or child to suffer rejection, pain, humiliation
And physical lashes at the hands of any man (or individual).
God made marriage to be a give and take of loving, respecting, and sharing as well.
Communication is essential, so it's comprising
That there is a fifty-fifty decision balanced enough to bring a resolution.
I've been hurt, I know; sometimes it's hard because those episodes keep coming back.
I admit I get upset but I have to let go and let God, for he is in charge.
I am sorry for feeling angry and I apologize for my mistakes.
Sorry, Lord, I will not let it happen again.
I am a stronger woman now and even if I stay poor, I will be at peace within myself.
I pray for forgiveness; I forgive my ex-husband.
Lord, grant me the serenity to accept the things I cannot change….

I Lived the Cycle of Turmoil

I

I lived the cycle of turmoil like a roller coaster
My life went up and downhill
I never knew what to expect him to do or say
Because his moods were unpredictable
His coercion, threats, and intimidation
Made me feel like crumbling
For I never knew what to expect
Or what day it would happen
I felt I was walking on eggshells

He never acknowledged my emotions, nor did he empathize with me
It was always put-downs; playing mind games was his best
He often told me that no one would want me or care for me ever
For I one day would end up all alone because
I refused to put up with his abuse

He always blamed me and told me that I was at fault
I always did wrong things, never right in his eyes
He would tell my children, "Look your mother is crazy"
Tears would fall down from my eyes and sadness would reflect in theirs

He felt that he deserved the best and was superior to us all
He always needed to have quiet at every movement at the dinner table
He would look for an excuse to fight at times
Even when things went right
It was just a runaway roller coaster riding high

The ups came with a period of honeymoon where he would be calm
But then the downs came and a storm would erupt
But in between there was a peak of tension rising high
Where he would act so moody and his irritability would skyrocket
Then all of a sudden a volcano would explode
My roller coaster would come crashing into a dead-end zone
No one could have saved me unless I saved myself
Back and forth we went
On and off it went
I tried leaving many times

But his guilt trips forced me to change my mind
For he brought me down so badly that it was hard to understand
That this was all his doing and the fact that he wouldn't change

II

For one day my roller coaster got stuck someplace up on the top
I was able to see the skies and sun shining bright
I realized then that I should no longer take
The misery he'd given, together with all the pain
For I felt trapped on the top of the hill
Did not know how to come down
I cried for help but no one was around
Felt alone and ashamed about life
I felt like a failure, for I could not comfort myself

For he was never my husband
He was my enemy instead, for how could you trust someone
Who lashes out of anger, scares away your security?
He was an abuser and a wife beater
His excuse was always, "You made me do it
If you wouldn't say, do, look, ask, or expect
I would not dislike you so much"

For in his eyes, you could see the deceit
And lies of a philandering man
Never did I ever feel secure in the arms of this man
I always felt that other women were
Always present with us even in our intimacy
I felt them looking anxiously
Nothing was obscure
Everything came to light
For his double life came out

I realized that we were never going to make him happy
For no one makes anyone happy
It's something you must do for yourself
We could not satisfy his ugly nature
Nor could we be accepted
For everything we did was bad in his game

For we were hated for ruining his plight in life
And he despised the fact that he was a married man
His insecurity was at an all-time high
The family was just an obstacle for him
We stood in front of him as distractions for his lies to tell
Other women only knew the stories he had told them instead

III

Until one day I was enlightened and started to see the light
For I was no longer blind by his anger and control
Nor did I feel afraid of all his hostile behavior
I told myself, "Hey, I do not need to take this anymore"
I should be free as a bird who's been inside a cage for many years
After many tries of cutting loose I finally succeeded
For one day I got the strength to say, "It's over"
The shadow of darkness that was hovering was raised
And the light came inside my spirit and my life seemed uplifted

For who can live their whole lives
Getting their spirit crushed
Having their emotions and feelings ignored
Not being able to say what you feel
Nor even making decisions at someone else's will?
For control is it such a small word
But the damage it can cause is immeasurable
For in life we were not meant to be slaves
or to have to succumb to sleeping next to our enemy

I soon learned that there are others
Whose plights were in much greater disorder
And that this behavior and pattern
Is a cycle called violence
For I did not know I was not his property
Or his possession
I was a woman born to be free
To be treated with respect
To be loved for being me
To be able to stand on my own two feet

Be free to make my own decisions
Open to say what I feel I need to say
But not to experience any pain
At the hands of any man

I became stronger and set myself free
A new life I began and I followed a new script
Free to be me and love life again
For I am a survivor, a survivor of pain
A new purpose in life was given to me
I am number one; no one should make me feel less
For I won the race and the set has been broken
My roller coaster got there first....

The Life and Times of a Domestic Violence Victim

Count the minutes; count the hours until he gets out of work
Nervous stillness, tension rising, he will be home to stay
Tried to keep myself under control but my knees still shake
Keeping cool to avoid his storm, but sometimes it does not work
He comes in; instead of hi, looks at you deep in your eyes
With hatred so powerful your heart feels heavy
And beats loudly like the sound of a drum

His screams and shouting start without any warming
Cannot stop them, cannot block them—it's echoing so darn loud
Block myself, make believe I can't hear instead
Disassociate myself from his screams
I am so far gone that my mind starts to fly
If I am cooking, I will burn myself
If I am washing dishes, things start falling to the floor
If I am cleaning and paid him no mind,
He will make a bigger mess in front of my eyes
Leave it there for me to clean!

Dinner is finished, no thanksgiving prayer
Demanded silence; no one was to make a sound
If dinner was not hot enough, drink not cold enough,
Kids not quiet enough, or he is just mad enough, all hell will break loose
Food flying from walls to floor
Table to kitchen, everywhere there is a spread of food
A new paint color every day
Who will clean it? Of course, it will be me
For he will say you made me angry
It is your fault!

Hours, days, months, and years, still it seems like life would drag
Nothing changes, no improvement; in fact, it has gotten so much worse
From the tantrums came the pushing, from the pushing
came the smacking, from the smacking came the hits,
from the hits came the kicks—never-ending cycle
Things broken all over the place, children crying all around us

Police were here once again
Dr. Jekyll is here to stay, threats of taking my children away,
Threats of making me want to stay
No escape, trapped in a cage like an animal I always felt

Couldn't talk or speak my mind; I never made any sense to him
If I tried to listen to him, he always said I was not
If I spoke loud enough he still could not hear me
If I tried to tell him that he was hurting me, he would not acknowledge
my pain
No emotional connection, could not even have a good conversation
No talk, no care, no love, only fear
Hard to breathe, hard to live—my heart beats
Panic strikes, no relief, no compromising
Why do I have to feel this way?
Never before knew of stress until I met him
Stress was my middle name

Time was passing by; the physical violence stopped for a while
Then the verbal accusations, fear, and intimidation
Belittling every move I made
Making me feel like nothing at all
Could not question him, could not even ask him of his whereabouts
He was never faithful or a loving husband
It was just a pretend situation
Pretend we are playing house, but you are just a slave in my home
I work hard every day but to him it was just a measly job
I did not deserve better than that in his eyes
Could never do better than him, for he was better than I was, as he will
say!

You are the problem, you are fat, and you are crazy
In fact, you do not know what you are saying!
Months and months kept passing by; how many other women will you
have?
Tired of suffering and humiliation, I started to see the light
Kept pushing myself to be set free
Studying hard to get a better job and come out of this rut
Once I did finish my degree, a good job I got, but to him it was not
Work on making my life better, with or without him I struggled

However, how wrong I have been to think that he would change
Years and years kept going on but no resolution to this marriage
institution

Finally, one day he left with someone else
Could she be the one that will help me be set free?
No respect for marriage, no respect for his wife
Living a double life right in front of my eyes
One day the evidence came into play
This was my only way to show the truth
Finally after all these years
Of coming and going
Of leaving and returning
Of disappearing and reappearing
Of fights, arguments, shouts, and screams

Finally, life changed for me
And I had gained my freedom like a prisoner who's just been set free
With my freedom came the pain of knowing
I survived not just the marriage
Nevertheless, I have managed to save my life
For if years were to continue in this trap
One day it would have been too late for me
For I would have been dead instead
I would not been able to say I survived
The life and times of a victim of domestic violence

Words

Words can't hurt you or break you like the phrase states
Depending how you address them
They can do much more damage than you expect
I know; I am living example, proof of it, and knowledge of it

Words do hurt!
Take a child, for example, who
Has always been told, "You are no good" or
"You are stupid" all of their lives
What do you think this child will feel when he gets older?
There are many living proofs in shelters, foster care, and jails
That words do hurt
Just look around—you will see

Break you?
Not really? Words can't break you?
Take an abused woman who constantly hears demeaning words
Day in and day out
Trying to phase it all out
But the words ring like loud bells in the head
No matter how hard they try to shut it out
The words they still hear loud and clear
Often reliving the impact that they have left
Break you? They do, for they bring down the spirit

Demeaning words are tough to swallow
Demeaning words make stab wounds in the heart and soul
That no bandage can cover, no medicine can heal
Open wounds left with ooze of pain

Imagine being constantly put down, challenged, threatened, and cursed
Living life like an animal in a cage
Prisoners of words of intimidation and insecurities
Trying to get control by belittling others with words
Trying to feel superior by minimizing others with words
Trying to get results by using words that cause fear
Trying to manipulate by using paradoxical words to play mind games

Break you

They can if you let them—that's is what self-centered individuals say
Reality is that words do hurt and break the spirit
No human being deserves to be mistreated
No human being deserves to be called names
No human being deserves to be scarred in childhood
By the abusive words coming out of the mouths of their own parents
Words do hurt
Think before you speak and hurt an important person
Don't try to control others with words
Use kind words instead
You will get much more accomplished
Words with kindness have better results

Like a Caged Bird That Sings

Courageous me, brave at heart
Lonesome dove
Of this earth
Trapped in a cage
No way out
No escape
See the outside
Hope to be set free
Bondage, stillness happens
Food and water
For a bird to feed on
Courageous me, brave at heart
Sing my lonely song this morn....
Early wake up
Look outside
Knowing that I could not be free
The spring comes
Flowers bloom
Sun that shines
But still no way out

The summer has passed
Early autumn leaves turn dark green
I see them fall to the ground, slowly fading into the roadway
Wish that I could at least touch one

The early frost knocks at my door
Feel the chill of the cold air
My feathers thicken to keep me warm
But how I hope to be outside
Touch the snow
Feel the white
Feel the icy cold snow on the ground
Cold, windy, storms ahead
And still I wish I could be set free
Maybe if I sing a song
Loud and clear for all to hear
This caged bird can be set free

Claribel Coreano

And finally after all my years
Fly high into the skies
And sing so freely
This caged bird was me
Until I was set free
Like a caged bird that sings for new beginnings

Love Heals All Things …

I heard once that love heals all things
But I ask
Does it erase the pain caused by a man with cruel intentions?
Does it erase the misery of a lover's rejection?
Does it erase the lashes, the screams, or the pushes by the hands of your
man?
Does it erase deception, betrayal, and infidelity of a philandering man?
Does it erase the lies, scorns, and disrespect of how he treated you?

Or is it that as years go by your memory starts to fade
And you no longer remember those disturbing memories?
Or is it that finding a new love can make you forget?
Or is it that by reaching new heights of spirituality it can make them
disappear?
Or is it by loving yourself instead which makes it all clear?

Love does heal all things, for it is in love that we find healing
When we are in love it makes us act silly; you become numb to pain
Love does heal all things; true love is the miracle cure
To love unconditionally is to be patient, understanding, warm, loving,
optimistic
True love does heal; it inspires new hopes, new dreams, new goals
And your heart soon recovers from a past history of grief

And a new lease on life therefore begins
Hoping, yearning, wishing, loving, and waiting for a brighter future
Love does heal all things
For my heart had been broken, seeping hurts from the past
Brokenness, humiliation, and betrayal had torn my heart to pieces
It has slowly begun to heal by using my own home remedy
I started to love myself first
I accepted all the pain
I forgave all my trespassers
And became my own friend

Love healed my broken heart and taught me to be patient
It taught me to love others
And to use my energy to help the broken of spirit
Love healed all my sorrows
My misery is forgotten
The past is in the past, for I cannot remember it
The present I look forward to with acceptance every day
The future doesn't scare me anymore
Because of what I believe
With love you can conquer all....

Things I Have Learned About …

Authentic Love

What is genuine love? It is the ability to first love yourself,
acknowledging your true self and true identity,
accepting yourself as you are, and accepting others entirely.

Friendship first, which creates a bond of pure, spiritual unity,
it allows you to express yourself in a straightforward manner
without any hesitation,
learning to share with another,
creating a distance until you are willing to share the space.

Express yourself in kindness, which is the authentic power of love,
the truth in action which sets you free.
Be kind with each other, always expressing warmth.

Cherish each other's dreams,
honoring each other's dreams in reverence for each other.
Contribute to your individual goals equally, so both can benefit from
them.

Listen to what the heart is revealing,
which is the utmost level of cherishing an individual.
Pay attention to each other's emotions, feelings, and worries,
expressing what you are feeling and what you have to say.

Don't lock it up inside your heart; let it out.
You never know what answers you may find.
Remember, two heads are better than one.
Communication is the key to understanding
each other equally.
Intimacy is essential; set time aside for each other
to share intimacy in your own time and freedom.
Learn to give pleasure to each other and make love instead of sex,
for love making is the art of conveying your feelings.
It is not a means of alleviating tension;
it is a way two individuals come together in harmony,
committed to each other in a loving way,
setting the atmosphere, making it comfortable and beautiful
for both souls to share its energy.

Respect each other's wants and needs,
as long as they're valued mutually.

Maintain an equal awareness of each other.
Make it the golden rule: treat one another
as you would like to be treated.
No one is superior or lesser in decision making.
Both opinions count; just learn to compromise.
Don't argue over meaningless things.
It wastes too much energy.

Share without inhibitions; learn to be open.
Be open-minded and avoid being judgmental as well.
Always know that there are days we will get on each other's last nerve.
The important thing is to learn how to cope with each other's
personalities and maintain a sense of space.

To be available to do the things you like to do individually,
allow the respect to honor all self-interests and hobbies
that were there before we decided to share our time and space,
but come back in harmony and connect again with each other
in order to prevent certain conflicts to develop,
reassuring the other person that he/she is still loved.

Respect yourself first and your partner as well.
Be faithful always; be true to yourself.
Remember, once you fail it opens up a wound,
a wound that doesn't heal with a bandage.
As a result, lack of trust moves stealthily in
then it is hard to keep respect,
for if you failed by breaking the bond of trust
forgiveness will be hard to achieve
and all could be lost.

To be a companion, partner, friend, and lover is the ultimate goal.
How amazing will it be to share my life with the love of my life.
I know that I am preparing myself for something so awesome and
amazing,
because I know my partner is getting ready for me as well.
I can't wait to be his forever and wake up by his side.
I know it takes time to learn how to love but I wish it could be soon,

for I miss him so much and there is so much I want to share.
Genuine love comes from the heart, mind, and soul.
Please be there for me; time is getting short....

Real Intimacy

Intimacy
is to love heart to heart
to envision love, mind to mind
and to connect soul to soul
That is what real intimacy is all about

Genuine love
is being in the light
to shine and be yourself
Be open to let others know you
Don't let pride, frustration, or lack of patience
stop you from being genuine

Your Mind & Heart
Open your mind and heart like a crystal door
so clear and free to see right through you
Have reverence for each other
because we are spiritual beings
in search of growth
Allow to dream and share
your goals with each other

Forgive
Always learn to forgive and forget
Don't let mistakes and errors
build a wall in your way instead
Overcome with a simple
"I am sorry, please forgive me"
Learn to accept the apology
no matter how hurt you've been
For it is in forgivness that love grows instead

Forget
Because during the time you
refuse to forgive, the relationship grows weaker
instead of getting stronger
To forgive: it does not mean you are a powerless individual
It means you are a spiritual human
who is not afraid to grow

Communication

Communicate all your fears, dreams, anxieties,
and voice it so I can hear
I might be the listening ear
you have been waiting for
I will listen with my heart open
I will encourage you if you let me
I will be your support
when in doubt or fear
I will always be there to listen to you

Emotions/Feelings

For how will I know when you are feeling down?
When insecurity has dragged you down
a spiral of conflicts has left your brain twisted
and lost in confusion
Your thoughts are racing, thinking it is not worth it
Give up already; it's not worth the stress
For whoever heard that love has to hurt?
You never expected to find
someone who loves you
with their heart, mind, and soul

Believe

Never thought it could happen for real
Now you have it and you do not know how to care
Trapped in fear of commitment, your mind
is swirling, thinking it's safe to lose it

Don't Be Selfish

She will wait in space for your return
However long it takes me, I will come back
What a mistake to think of such
Why be so vain and selfish
in thinking only of yourself?
Whatever happened to me?

Don't Lose It

A good woman could never be cheated
For in heart she will see it
No need to play the games people play
For in life one day you will be a pawn
Like a chess game you will be played
Who will win, no one knows
Who is to say anyone wins when love is lost?

<u>My Strange Marriage Vows ...</u>

I take thee, the love of my life, to have and to hold until death do us
part ...
To love, to cherish, and to be faithful for the rest of my life.
But what if ...

I love you?
Will you love me forever, even when my skin sags...?
But please don't complain when I am too fat.

I will love you when you are a grouch,
But will you put up with me after a PMS fight?

I will take care of you when you feel ill,
But who's bringing me tea when I am in bed sick?

I will listen to you and share all your dreams,
But will you hear me when I tell you my goals, even if they stink?

I will encourage, motivate, and push you to succeed,
But will you share your achievements with me when you accomplish
financial success?

Or will you run off with a stranger
Who does not have to put up with all those days of you coming home
so late,
And not a kiss or a hug or a how was your day?

I will be faithful because my love is true,
But will you fall into temptation at the drop of a dime,
Just by a neighbor saying hi?

Or will I be the woman of your dreams for only a short time?
Will you desire others as time goes by
Or will you accept us growing old together?

What if ...
There are tears on my pillow
Burning with sorrow from your doing?

I will certainly let you know
If you have broken my heart,
Which was not part of the contract—did you forget that?

What if ...
I decide enough is enough,
No pain no more suffering
Am I willing to take by the man who is
Supposed to be my best friend.

What if I decide ...
Forget the till death do us part
And ask you to give me the keys to my heart?
The lock is now closed and you can't understand why.

Please go on your way.
I can no longer bear the stench of yourself.
I can no longer be the woman who shares
Her love with you, not after all this.
Please don't be so naïve.

For I am not going to stay,
Tolerating any bullshit.
I hope that you know
That is not part of the agreement
I once had promised in that "till death do us part" bit.

My vows still stand
And it does not specify any maltreatment should be accepted.

No clause or amendment that states
A phrase such as this: "You should take everything
From your partner but you may never leave...."

Therefore, I will stick to my own version
And if I have to spell it out for you I will,
But remember there is no turning back.
Take it or leave it.
This is just me ... I know what I want.
Can you hear me out, please?

Faithfulness

I

The secret to a long-term relationship is faithfulness and dedication to
grow....
Values and morals are in the rings of commitment to a happy
relationship.
To have loyalty you need to let yourself be guided
by the golden rule of partnership.

To learn to grow with the other person spiritually,
to be a faithful person, one must really know themselves enough
to be able to resist temptation and not give in to a moment of desperation.
To know how much you appreciate your partner,
remembering not to cause them any sorrow by your selfishness,
remember that God sees everything and there is nothing to hide,
for one day you will need to be prepared when it all comes to light....
To think of him/her at all times, even when they disappoint you,

And always to be able to express what it is that instigates the reaction,
To be able to share about your day even when you think
he/she might not want to pay attention.
You will soon find out that
he/she might want to listen and share equally too.
Remember always that communication is the key
that connects two individuals at times when things go wrong
and at times when things go right.

II

To be able to say, "I am sorry," when you are wrong
and accept your mistakes, but not forget to compromise as well.
When you lose interest in the other person, try hard
to think of the first time you met them; you will see that the feelings
are still there, you just need to light the spark,
set the fire of romance, bring it to light.
Remember we grow old and change our ways of accepted wisdom,
but when two souls are connected,
you will see that communication has grown
and both can even tell what each other is thinking!

Remember the love that brought you two together,
so pure and sacred,
When a union of two souls which were meant to be destined.
Cherish the person who gives their unconditional
love to you at all times,
remember that a unique person like that is hard to find;
don't throw away a beautiful thing that exists
between two individuals
who found each other amidst life's turmoil
and found peace within each other's arms,

the one thing they had been searching for all their lives.
Don't throw it away to start with someone new,
thinking this could happen again, for there is no guarantee.

III

Think of all the good things this person is all about;
forget their faults and weakness.
Remember that you too have them
and that he/she might feel the same way about you,
So how can you be faithful to the one that truly deserves the respect?
Remember, if you fall into sin and you do it anyway,
things may never be the same.
Trust will be lost and love will be diminished,
for betrayal exterminates all the years of hard work
you have put into the relationship,
in order to have gained the confidence that once existed.
Deception and betrayal are destroyers of the bond,
the bond that once held you together and that now seems to be gone....

So how can you prevent it?
Be true to yourself and be true to them.
Love yourself enough to love him/her as well.
Be secure enough to be a man/woman of conviction and say, "No,
I have someone who loves me and doesn't deserve this shame;
therefore, I must go to the one I love and give him/her all my love...,"
to all of those who believe in being faithful....

Integrity

The truth will set you free: it's a phrase as old as the end of time
What is the truth?
To be true you need to practice what you preach
Be honest at all times
Let others know what they are doing wrong
As well as accepting when you are reprimanded
Truth, honesty, integrity are all loaded words
That go hand in hand in life
To be an honest person there are no holds barred
You will state the truth no matter how hard

A person of integrity does not hide away from the truth
Integrity means living your life in honesty, in all areas of your life

For what good is it having an excellent position or status quo
But when you are with your family you are abusive?

For what good is it having come from a wealthy family
But you have selfish pride and act in arrogance towards others?

For what good is it pretending to be something you are not
Just to please others?

Integrity means not living a double life
Integrity means not abusing your family
Integrity means communicating with honesty
Integrity means becoming aware of others' plight
Integrity means not living your life recklessly
Integrity means not lying, cheating, and misleading
Integrity means not obtaining things through manipulation and deception
Integrity means not abusing your body, which is your temple
By using drugs, irresponsible sex, and other thoughtless ventures
Integrity involves many areas of life
It is not just saying, "I am a person of integrity"
But by showing it in the way you live your life
RESPONSIBILITY for your actions
Responsibility to others
Responsibility to society

And responsibility to God
The truth will set you free ...
As it is written by me....

<u>Parenting</u>

Not everyone is fit to be a father or a mother
A father is supportive of all his sons and daughters
A father is patient with his children even when his patience is running thin
A father shows love even when he is feeling alone
A father listens to his children when they need him
A father provides comfort when the child is afraid
A father provides guidance when the child is confused
A father provides financially for his family
A father accepts his lot in life and accepts his responsibility
A father sticks around until his children are all grown
A father waits for the day his children graduate from university
A father counts the days to see when his son or daughter is to get married
A father cannot wait to be a grandfather
A father is there until he breathes his last breath

A real father is not selfish
A real father is not arrogant
A real father does not run away and abandon his family
A real father does not strike his son or daughter because he is angry at world
A real father does not avoid responsibility
A real father does not hide his financial worth to his family
A real father does not think of himself first and create his own agenda
A real father does not belittle or use demeaning words with his children
A real father does not ignore his children even when he does not live with them
A real father does not forget he is a father until his death
A real father does not forget that a real father is the one who sticks around
A real father does not forget that before he became a father he had a father himself
A real father does not repay his children for all the pain that his own father gave him
A real father lets go of all his childhood dysfunction
A real father creates wonderful memories for his children
A real father learns to forgive and forget all who done him wrong
A real father inspires hope and love to his children
A real father is the inspiration of God's own love for us

What father gives his children a rock
When they are hungry asking for bread?
Remember that you will be old one day
The father title would not matter much
If your own children would not be by your side
When you are facing death all alone with no one there to console and
comfort you
Remember that you will be there one day
Moreover, yearn for the love you missed out on instead
Cry the tears of death, for there will not be a son or daughter by your bed
Don't die alone; learn to love
Learn to lead by example
Teach your children well and in your life you will be blessed.

What Does a Homeless Person Look Like?

What does a homeless person look like?
Do they wear raggedy clothes, look dirty, hair frazzled, and carry many bags?
Do they sleep in the streets or inside their cars with blankets
and pillows to help them sleep right?
In fact, do they walk around with a backpack carrying their toothbrush
and one pair of clothes?

Do they always look sick and out of control?
Do they look crazy and incoherent like so many say?
Do they always sleep in a cardboard box, under highways or
park benches in nights that are cold?
Are they unable to work or make ends meet?

Misconceptions in life it must seem,
for I have seen them in many different circumstances.
Homelessness does not carry its own characteristics
or a gene that distinguishes a homeless person from another individual.
For they are Blacks, Whites, Hispanics, Europeans, and from many other nations.
I have met them disabled, handicapped, or psychiatrically troubled.
I have met them with no schooling, some college, having a bachelor's,
and some even have master's as well.

Some are from good families, some are not.
Moreover, some do not have any support at all.
Some come from wealth, others are poor,
and some are just going in cycle they never will cure.
Some because of liquor, drugs, or criminal activity ended up without a home.
Some lost their middle-class, white-collar, or executive jobs and ended
up losing everything they had.

Some are running away from themselves.
Some are running away from their mate.
Some are running away from the law.
Some are running away from God.
Some are running away from reality.
Some are just hiding for no one to find them.
Some are running from it all.

Some are single with no one to help them.
Some are married with many problems.
Some are single mothers/fathers with children fending for themselves.
Some are from very large families not able to make ends meet.
Some are from abusive families.
Some are from a domestic violence situation, running away from their
perpetrator.

Homelessness does not discriminate because of age, beauty, or
intelligence.
I have seen those old, young, middle aged.
Some I have seen since birth and stayed long enough to say their first
words.
What can we do to help the homeless?
Remember they are just like you and me.
They could be someone in your family.
Can you imagine having it all and then having it all taken away?
How would you feel to find yourself out in the streets?
Nowhere to go, no one to help,
not even a blanket on a cold, rainy day.

Whenever you see someone carrying a sign that says, "I am hungry,"
or, "Will work for food,"
remember that they are just like you and me.
Circumstances have taken a toll
and nomads in a homeless culture they have become.
Help them get out of the rut; don't let them sink in even deeper, lost
without hope.
Reach out to them; inspire some trust.
Show them some faith and tell them God loves them instead.
Teach them the skills to survive in this world.
Do not mock or reject them
or leave them alone; they have experienced it all.

For those whose addictions have destroyed all of their hopes?
Do not give up on them, because they have already done so.
Instead, let them see that for once in their lifetime
someone has not given up on them.
It is hard to admit that homelessness does not have only one face
but a heart, soul, and a spirit as well.

Share the love of God with those of weak spirit; share hope and a
positive future.

Wisdom

Wisdom is gained by all the years of suffering
We live life going through many different stages
A journey of accomplishments, difficulties, trials, and tribulations
At times we are not fully aware of how to react to the many different
circumstances
We later learn that there were many hard lessons to learn
Looking to the past only brings tears of regret
Remember only the wonderful memories in its place
Having survived a life of adversity makes a person more interesting
Having a story to share and tell to others
Can help an individual with their own troubles

Being wise comes with experience
Knowledge is not book learned
It is living through it
Intelligence is the versatility of knowing many different things
Patience is gained not through genetic encoding
Patience is developed from many different situations
Perseverance comes with the instinct of not giving up
Respect is not earned through intimidation or fear
Respect is earned by what you teach others
Gratitude is giving for all you have gained in life
Sharing of yourself with love in your heart
The spirit knows how to judge a character
The spirit knows how to differentiate what is good and what is evil
Being self-conscious is to think before you act
Instinct can help you make choices deep inside your heart
When you feel something is not right, it most likely is not
When you feel a good feeling inside, something good is coming your
way
Being positive is not stating it but making it happen
Running away from problems does not make them go away
Confront them with a passion that nothing can get in your way
Everyone has been born to make an impact on this world
Sooner or later you too will make an impression on somebody
And help them learn their lessons in life
Your purpose in life only God knows
Be open to learn all the lessons life has to offer

Claribel Coreano

True wisdom is acceptance of others and yourself
Acceptance of all your life mistakes
Acceptance of all the good things to come
Wisdom is respect, integrity and understanding of life

Nature

The Sea So Purifying and Mysterious

The sea so purifying and mysterious
can cleanse the soul without any effort
The solemn balance of the waves soothes the spirit
to control human emotions left untouched
The beauty and splendor of its beauty remind us of a higher power
to think of how your life could be and how you're spending every hour
And if by chance you get to see a sunrise in the ocean
it feels like a renewal of hope to see a brighter day
And if you see a sunset in the ocean it can help you
let go of all the pain

Respect its inhabitants because they can also teach a great lesson
How happy they are in their natural environment
and always thanking their Creator
For they don't fuss, complain, or even get depressed
that God has placed them there for us humans to be conscious of

Such a great gift from a Father, who loves us enough
to provide us with such splendor, the sea so vast
the deepness of how much he loves us
the strength of His words and the power to reach us
It's like a child who paints his first picture for his father
and is rewarded for its goodness
We are so blessed to be able to admire such magnificence
for I can imagine if I was blind
and not able to see it—how dark and sad that would be
not able to see the ocean

I reach for the sea to let go of my pain and call unto the waves
pray that in my life I could be blessed
I speak to God because the ocean is like an instant messenger
It's an information source to reach the Lord effectively
The winds in the sea are just God's caresses
gently telling me, "My child, everything is going to be all right.
Walk the shores, don't be afraid,
let go of everything,
and I will lead you to higher grounds.
For even the birds announce me every morning,

and all creation praises me.
Be thankful for the ocean,
for I gave it to free you."

A Butterfly Flies Towards the Wind ...

A butterfly flies towards the wind, flies high in the clear blue skies with a
gleam
Wings wide open to endure the wind, fly high, let it soar, reach the zenith
See the beauty of the scenes, see the wildflowers, fly in circles
Look at how the wind makes them swing from side to side
The sun shines and lights the path, the warmth of a clear, hot summer day
Imagine the feeling of such flight; feel the wind, feel the beauty on your
skin
See the colors; red, yellow, blue, and orange
A kaleidoscope of colors you can see from afar
Fly high, fly high

See the green grass in the valley below, see the peak of the mountaintops
See the rivers, and see the lakes; I will follow nature's trail
Stop to notice the forests, admire the trees, and touch the leaves
See their schemes of colors, hues of green, yellow, and brown
Say hello to the trees; they are older than you and me
Feel the moisture and warmth of the forest
See the flowers that live in the care of Mother Nature's forests
Roam the valleys, roam the streams
See nature's beauties yell out, "Take care of me
I cannot manage it alone; respect life and respect me"
Remember to keep it clean
So that other generations
Can have a high regard for nature's gifts

Follow the streams that lead to the rivers,
Follow the rivers that lead to the ocean
Come to the ocean when you need a direct line to speak to God
Feel the waves, hear the sounds, smell the tranquility, in its entirety
Say a prayer; you will see that the ocean is the closest link
To God's line, an instant message He will receive
For the ocean is immensely full of life's mysteries

A great link to you and me
Let loose of all your worries while at sea
Let the waves carry it out to the deep ocean; it knows how to transmit it
out

Let the closeness to your beginnings help you reach life's understanding
Let it take you, let it leave you in touch with your spirituality

Thank you, Lord, for the ocean; it cleanses the soul, aligns the spirit
Gives you hope for the future, and high regard for your surroundings
Like a butterfly I fly high, so high in the sky I can see the sun going
down
As the sun is going down, hues of colors light up the skies
Go down slowly, night skies set in
A dark, clear night starts settling in
Stars shining bright light up the skies: stars to north and stars to the south
Beautiful designs go east and west
Leaving their glow as they fly by
Reach for the stars, aim high
The moon lights up the universe softly, luminary hues of gray
So big and bold leading light
Like a big eye standing out in the skies
Everything in the earth is connected to the gravity of the shiny moon
Even the ocean waves receive vibrations from the moon's own gravity

Perhaps it's a 911 call to the heavens being placed in desperation
For God to hear, shake the heavens, reach the throne
Amazing skies, clouds of rain, and cloudy night began to display
No one knows what the thunder and lightning's function really is
Thunder and lightning sound as if God is crying or stomping on the
ground
I do wonder when it takes place if He is joyful or if He is irate
I question when it rains if the rain is God's tears instead
Is he shedding tears of joy or tears of sadness?
Crying for the world to search for Him?
Rain is cleansing; let it wash out all your pain from the past
Just like a cloudy day turns into light

But the signs that God is real are not to be ignored
The signs are visible in nature and in its beauty
The skies are a witness; the sea is part of us
The earth was the first ingredient He used when he molded all of us
And nature is a flower garden He made especially for us
Imagine a world empty, empty without this beauty to love
Where will you go to see an ocean?
Where will you go to see a mountain?

97

Valleys and streams?
No picture will come to your mind
Remember to appreciate all He's given you
Be thankful for all!

For what father can afford such a significant present for his sons/
daughters
Of giving you a universe to explore and to be indebted for?
Rivers, lakes, oceans, skies, forests, mountains, and valleys
All great wonders of a beautiful artist who has left His mark
For all to wonder at and admire
A work of art so miraculous no one else can reproduce it
For He made it especially for you
Like a butterfly flies towards the wind
I will continue on my life's journey
For God has let me see that I am not an insignificant thing
I am as special as all creation....

I See a Brighter Future…

I see a brighter future even though it is a cloudy day.…
I see a rainbow in the sky
even when I feel like crying and shedding tears like the rain.…

I see a brighter future in spite of all the pain my heart has felt.
I keep my head up and pretend that all is well
even though my heart aches.

I see a brighter future even when no one is around
to help me through my difficulties and to show me comfort
when I'm feeling all confused.

I see a brighter future when I am alone in my bed
and no one is around me to hold me.
But I know that God is in control.

I see a brighter future even when I have lost all will to fight.
I push myself and find a little spark of faith
which lifts me up and makes me strong.

I see a brighter future even when I'm feeling weak
and no one is here to fend for me when I am feeling sick.
I only pray for God's comfort to let me see yet another day!

For in my life I have had my share of pain.
I still need to see a brighter future because I see that I am not alone,
that there are others whose plight in life is much more severe.

I see a brighter future and thank God that I am alive!
I praise His name and say,
Lord, you know the plans and you will be my guide.

I see a brighter future because I have known God's love from close up.
His hands are holding mine
and walking me through all the difficult patches of my life.

His mercy has shown me to be patient,
His love has made me grow,
and sharing His love with others whose pain could be much worse.

I now know how great is my God, for he has made me
strong, wise, and glad to be alive.
In spite of everything I have lost, great blessings will come my way.
For his words are never in vain;
he has promised me a miracle,
and a miracle I claim.
I know that he will me make see a brighter day
each and every day.

Reach for the Stars

Reach for the stars no matter how high
Every step will take you closer
To those dreams that are far to reach
Imagine you can touch them, imagine they are definite
For by trying every time you soon will learn a trick or two
To help you gain new skills to learn the ins and outs
For every time you fail at something
Just keep your head up high
And just get up
Try, try all over again

Reach for your dreams when it is feasible to make them come true
Don't wait till your're old to rush them
Remember, some things are to be done early in life
For you do not want to appear like a fool in disguise
You cannot cheat time nor can you make it wait for you
Life goes by in stages; don't get stuck in a phase
Trying hard to get away in haste

Realize goals that can be measured
Find a solution to a problem
Compromise enough to get you there
Accept the unacceptable and keep going
Don't let go of or push away love
For this might be the only way to reach it
Remember, in life everything is meaningless
Without the source that makes sense
The lamp to guide you and shine right through
So you can see the obstacles in your way
Remember, without God, love, and peace
We are nothing even if we reach
For if we get there on empty
No power source left to help you
And no emergency backup to restore you
You will be alone, alone in space
Flying high to reach
A runaway star in a never-ending universe

The Storm

Calm winds, warm air softly blowing in the square
Skies of blues turn into grays
Slowly changing into darker grays
Dark clouds forming
No stars in sight
No sun to shine
Just stillness of the calmness
Of the stirring of the storm
With great force it comes
With strong winds it surrounds us
With powerful annihilation
It is Mother Nature
Source of energy recharges in the sea
Comes back in the form of a hurricane
Some named Frances, Charley, and Ivan
Do not forget Jeanne is also coming
It seems that they are in a competition
Of which one can cause the greatest demolition
Winds come forcefully
Rain pours vigorously
Hissing of the winds
Chilling sounds of enraged nature
Darkens the day
Swells up the rivers
Stirs up the oceans to rise above earth
Trees fall all over the roads
Branches lay in the grass to wither
Storm ceases all of a sudden
Silent recovery bustling to the storm
Winds slows so quietly
Warmth is felt in the air
Aftermath destruction is everywhere
Homes smashed down
Roofs have flown to another yard
Broken windows
Shattered dreams
My dream house no longer exists
Rebuild, Reclaim, and Reform

We all need to start to build up somehow
Everyone is occupied in cleaning up the mess left behind
Hope and pray another hurricane does not come our way
Stay away; keep on going your own way
We've had enough; we had plenty; you overstayed your welcome
Leave quietly
Leave quickly
Leave some tranquil winds behind
Mother Nature is demanding respect
Trying to catch our attention
That God is in control
And no one should question that
He allows it
He permits it
He commands it
Then so be it
Thank you, Lord
That the storm has ceased

Tears of Sorrow for Every Season

Seasons change like dead leaves; the past has died
A new beginning as springs arrives
New leaves it brings, new hope, new dreams

Tears of joy from my eyes flow
Like the brightness and the beauty of a shiny Spring day
The day I met you and the beginning of us
Tears of joy from my eyes flowed
As I thank God for meeting you
Tears flow for every day, night, month, and year
I have hoped to be close to you
Tears flow and flow

Seasons change like the flowers blooming
The grass is greener on the other side
As you perceive it
Colors of Summer start to come out
Tears of sorrow from my eyes flow
Like a river in a midsummer night
Knowing that you are no longer here
Tears flow to forget the grief of a lover's good-bye

Seasons change like the brown, greens, and yellow hues of Autumn
Darkening the path of what was to be
Leaving me with a torn heart from your deceit
Tears of sorrow from my eyes flow
Like raindrops falling in the leaves on a dark, windy Autumn day
Cold and warm tears flow, leaving puddles of water
In every dip, remembering us
Moreover, how much I miss you

Seasons change like the breeze coming through my window
The present is yours to have until the frost again arrives
My tears of sorrow flow like snowflakes in the Winter
Crystalize in a cold, Winter night
The stillness and frozenness of space portrays between us
Tears flow, letting me know what could have been
But you did not want to try

In hope of catching a glimpse of you
Fuzzy, shadowy figure of you
Hoping that it could be you I see

As the Winter creeps in and the snow starts to fall
Within each snowflake that falls to the ground
I make a wish that you can see that seasons change
Leaving time for spiritual growth
To see and analyze what we could be
Things that need to change in us

In hope of finding each other again in the Spring
For the future comes with the newness of leaving all behind
Starting again anew like nothing had ever happened between us
Like the flowers bloom in Spring
So will our love grow each season
As we grow old, we will reflect on the many seasons together
Thanking God for letting us find each other again
Tears of joy will flow from our eyes
When looking into each other's eyes again
Awaiting the different seasons, in each other's arms

I Saw the Sunrise Through My Window Today

I saw the sunrise through my window today
Light up the clear blues skies
Soft white clouds sparingly surrounded the sun
Skies of light baby blues with hues of yellow
And bright orange illuminating the skies in plain view of my eyes
Across the horizon in my vision I felt hope
Of a new beginning today

My eyes as clear as daylight saw a miracle take place
My heart felt the confirmation of knowing that you are okay
The closeness to nature and the beauty of creation
Gave me a clue that I will hear from you
It told me swiftly as if a wind passed by
Reassurance of the beauty of the spark
The light that still shines
The hope that does not give up
The miracle that will happen
The faith that does not cease
The wish to be near you
My friend, my lover, and my partner you will be

In hope that one day this beauty that I see
In the skies
In the seas
In the trees
In the leaves
In the butterfly that flies by
My love you will feel and witness

For you taught me to love nature
Within it I find closeness to you
It brings me one step closer
To feeling you next to me
Strange feeling of missing you
Left a tear in my eye
I was about to cry
When I saw the sunrise

Nature

I remember as a child how
close to nature I had been
I played with dirt
counted flowers
followed butterflies
played with bees
until I got stung

ate hibiscus if I got hungry
like an open faucet
drank from rain water
followed lizards, counted them
let them hang from my ears
They were my friends

Had ducks and a duck pond
watched them lay eggs
counted the families as they walked with grace
had goats
fed them grass
watched how funny they ate
pulled on their beard
just to see them
come strike at me

On a clear night
counted stars in the sky
stayed up to see if the earth
would move as the stars flew by

loved to play with leaves
made mountains and hills
threw myself into them
like swimming in a pool

Lady bugs were my favorites
Loved to watch them land on my hands
let them walk up my arms
said good-bye when they left

Slugs and snails
I kept in a bucket
put them in races
to see which one was fastest

Rain came
Raindrops fell like buckets
Under the waterspout
was my favorite spot
Let the rain pour down my head
like Niagara Falls
It was fun until
I got cold and purple

Summer days
were so amazing
Steaming hot during the days
walked barefooted
to feel the hot condensing rays
burn my soles to the ground

At night the floor became so cold
I loved to lay face down
to feel the coldness of the marble
Made believe it was a piece of ice

Almond tress, acerola, and tamarind
Papaya, guava, and guanabana
Fruits I used to steal
Eat as I walked by
got hungry
There I would pick
from a neighbors tree

To live with no worries
because nature took care of me
Happy child
in love with nature

Spanish Expressions
Part I El Comienzo de un Amor

La Primera Vez

Cuando te vi por primera vez
Quede pasmado ante la mirada y el dulce de tús ojos
Que brillan como piedra de cuarzo
Cuando los toca un rayo de sol
Creo que me temblaron las rodillas
Cada vez que tu mirada chocaba con la mía
No pude ni siquiera disimular

Mis ojos seguirán cada movimiento de tú cuerpo
Como una mariposa sigue una gota de agua
en el pétalo de una flor
Fue maravilloso
Eres como una fuente
natural de agua cristalina
Donde solo los atrevidos
y valientes podrán llegar
Si alguien me preguntaran como eres
Solo diré:
La Belleza, La Ternura, La dulzura
¡ Hecha mujer esa soy yo!

Mi Músico

Como una cuerda en tu guitarra
Sin tono y afinación así se encuentra mi alma hoy
Pues el músico quien tocaba su música fina que yo escuchaba
Con sus manos afinaba las cuerdas con amor
Hasta que de su ser se escuchaba una melodía
Con toda su alma y esfuerzos
Pensaba cual cuerdas tocar
Para que su música solo la escuchara yo
Y apreciaba cada tono y melodía

Mi músico con su guitarra tocaba canciones que traspasaban mi corazón
Sin èl todavía agregarle palabras a su melodías
Mi corazón entendía lo que el me decía
Entre los líricos que el tocaba yo sentía lo que el expresaba
Dolor profundo sentía con cada cuerda
Como si una historia estaba siendo narrada
Y yo era la única la cual entendió
Mi corazón a veces se sentía como estallar
Porque las fuerzas me faltaban para controlar lo que sentía
Y sin que el se diera cuenta yo me encogía
Y pretendía que nada sentía

Este músico con sus melodías mi corazón se ganó
Y tan triste y sola me dejado cuando todavía escucho su melodía
Ya el músico no toca su guitarra para mí
Las melodías que el tocaba ya no las toca para mi
Como una guitarra vieja en su cajeta yo he quedado
Puesta en una esquina en su recamara
Olvidada y con polvo encima
Ya se está poniendo vieja
Pues ya no tiene la atención del músico
Quien con gran amor le tocaba en su mejores años

Así sin imprevisto comparo yo lo que ha pasado
Mi músico me ha olvidado
Y ya sus melodías cual yo tanto apreciaba no las escucho
Son pocas las memorias que me quedan
Su silueta en un espejo todavía lo contengo

Su aparición veo y con sus finas manos tocando
Las cuerdas en su guitarra con tanto fulgor

Como si fuera en vida real lo cual me acuerdo
Pues es solo las memorias como un sueño
De un guitarrista quien conocí en el pasado
Y ni tan siquiera un adiós me dijo cuando se fue
Solo melodías en mis memorias escucho de vez en cuando
Deseando con todo cariño ver otra vez mi músico

Quien me robo mi corazón
Quisiera con toda mi alma poder oírle otra vez
Con una canción nueva de su corazón
Yo le daría toda mi atención
Para poder escuchar bien las melodías de su ser

La Bachata de Mi Vida

Tú viniste a mi vida,
En un tiempo cuando yo había perdido
Todo el ánimo de vivir,
Me proveíste una emoción con la esperanza de tener...
¡Alguien como tú!
Sin poder estar dispuesto a proveer...
Pretendiste sentir lo mismo que yo,
¡Ni si quiera supiste disimilar tu pretensión!
¿Porque? me pregunto?
Porque me diste falsas esperanzas
De que algún día tu amor podría conocer
Ni siquiera pensastes en mis sentimientos
Y fallastes cuando me rompistes mi corazón
Por tu falsedad y mentira.
Tú me has causado mucho dolor,
Y has hecho una herida en lo extremo de mi
Alma en tan poco tiempo.
Te pregunto ¿porqué? ¿Por que mi Amor?
¡Te has llevado contigo un trozo de mi corazón!
Espero ansiosamente poder oír tú voz,
Las horas pasan y no se si tú me deseas como yo a ti...
Anhelo el día cuando te tenga en mis brazos,
Y con fuerzas del alma abrazarte.
Espero pacientemente a escondidas
Y si oyeras mi corazón responderme,
Tú sabrás que en mis brazos hallarás amor y cariño.
Y si me rechazas algún día te arrepentirás Y será muy tarde para ti...
Pues quizás alguien más vendrá y de mi amor se aprovechará...
No sigas dudando y entrégate a mí...
Verás que los dos hallaremos la felicidad juntos
Y no te arrepentirás de conocer tu verdadero Amor

113

Como Hacerte Comprender

Mi amor, no se como hacerte comprender de que tú eres el amor de mi
vida
Cada cada día que pasa en vez de olvidarte te quiero más y más
Y anhelo con deseos locos, de estar entre tús brazos
Sentir tu calor y tú piel en mi pecho
El roció de tu abrazo y tús manos en mi cuerpo
Amándome con pasión sin ningún desprecio
Ver esos ojos de color obscuro, que me miren con atención y admiración
Tocar tú cuerpo como nunca tú hayas sentido
Besar tús labios color canela y tocar tú cabello castaño
Amor mío acércate a mi, no te alejes
No desprecies este amor tan puro y divino que te ofrezco
Con humildad y cariño
No me desprecies amor mío, antes que sea tarde
Tú verás que no te miento y es verdad que te amo y nunca te olvidare
Y pase lo que pase en mi corazón siempre estarán los dulces recuerdos
De un amor inevitable que nunca me supo responder.
Tú tomas un lugar especial en mi corazón

Ayer Creí Oír tu Voz

Ayer creí oír tu voz
Pero solo fue un recuerdo en el momento
Ayer creí sentir tus caricias
Pero solo fue el viento en un suspiro
Ayer creí ver tu sombra
Pero solo fue un extraño
Pasando en el camino

Ayer creí oír tu risa en mi oído
Pero solo fue la risa de un niño
Ayer creí sentir tu piel cerca de mí
Pero solo fue el abrazo de mi hijo
Ayer creí que te vi
Pero no fuistes tú vi solo la sombra de un amigo

Ayer creí oír que me llamaste
Pero no fuistes tú
Fue un extraño pasando por mi lado
Los tiempos de ayer han pasado
Aun tu ser sigue conmigo
Igual que ayer aún te amo
Igual que ayer me haces falta
Igual que ayer te sigo esperando
Igual que ayer deseo verte
Igual que ayer eres mi amigo
Igual que ayer te sigo amando

Tres Días

Han pasado tres días y ya no me buscas
Presiento que otro amor has conocido
Ahora ella tiene tu atención
Tú algún día sabrás que ella nunca era lo ideal
Sin embargo por tu orgullo a ella la escogistes
Y a mi me abandonastes por un capricho de amor.
Tu ego fue más fuerte que tú
Pues venció en convencerte que una
Mujer tan simple como yo no era para ti.
Que error mi amor…
Quizás algún día te des cuenta de tú error,
Y con un corazón quebrantado deseares mi amor.
Cuando llegé ese tiempo
Y despiertes de tú pasión por mí,
Sabrás que yo era la mujer ideal para ti.
Pero quien sabe si entonces
Tú no seas el hombre ideal para mí.
No esperes tanto tiempo para recobrar mi corazón,
Quizás ahora halla tiempo para salvar nuestro amor.

Mi Poemas del Alma

¡Hay si tú supieras como te quiero amor!
Te deseo con una fuerza dél alma
Y no estaré quieta hasta que te tenga y consumas este amor.
Amor como el mío nunca encontraras
Y no importa en quien y en cuantas lo busques
Amor, yo soy tuya,
¡Ámame como nunca has amado a otra mujer!
Has tú sueño realidad en mis brazos,
Te prometo que nunca te fallare
Y seré fiel hasta la muerte ya tú lo sabrás.
Mi amor sinceramente puedo declarar que te amo...
Te amo y no lo escondo ni tampoco lo niego
Y si lo tengo que declarar a todo el mundo lo haré.
Tú eres el hombre que amo,
El hombre que deseo,
El hombre que admiro
Y respeto con honor sin igual.
Que difícil saber que te quiero
Y tú ni siquiera los sabes.
Me atemoriza saber que no sientes lo que yo siento
Todos los días pasan
Y le pido a Dios que tan siquiera un poquito me puedas querer
Me conformo con nada mas tenerte en mis brazos una sola vez,
Y saborear tu amor piel a piel.
¿Como te explico lo que siento por ti?
Quizás soy muy romántica y nostálgica a la vez
Creyendo en un amor de larga distancia,
Sin saber cuales otras están a tu alcance
Y de mi ni tan siquiera te acuerdas
Ni tampoco respondes a mis sentimientos
mejor es no saber…
Hasta cuando podrás ignorar un amor como el mío,
Puro, sencillo y sin ningún reproche
¡Que espera pacientemente tu repuesta!
¿Nunca llega a mi ni tan siquiera una chispa de un si o no?
Por favor decídete
Déjame seguir mi largo camino
Rumbo a mi meta
Tal vez en mi jornada te encuentre otra vez.

¿Dónde Estas Mi Corazón?

¿Amor mío, dónde estas? no sabes la falta que tu presencia me hace,
Me duele en saber que me ignoras por puro capricho
Y que te niegas a ti mismo, Que no me quieres por tu propio despecho
Yo no puedo negar, que estoy enamorada y te deseo con pasión
inesperada
¡Si es un amor improvisado, que yo misma no estaba preparada para
recibir,
¡Y aun lo esperaba!
Pero desafortunadamente a mí llego
No se que decir y como expresar lo que siento…
Yo sé que tu no sientes lo mismo que yo, y ha causa de esto te has
alejado de mi
Por miedo de también caer en las redes de este amor
Que lentamente fue creciendo en mi corazón,
Que nada más oír tú voz, te sentía cerca de mí,
tu manera de hablar me hace sentir como si estoy a tu lado
Para convivir un amor puro y hermoso
Cual no puedo definir ¿por que a mi?
¿Por que ahora?,
¿Y por que fuisteis tú?
Quien tocó mi alma y ha perturbado el balance perfecto de mi diario
vivir.
Yo no puedo esperar más,
Me sucumbo por poder estar un día a tú lado
Y amarte lentamente hasta salir el sol y recibir de ti con el mismo
fulgor la pasión interna de este amor…

Te Busco

¿Donde esta mi corazón?
Te busco y no te encuentro
Te escondes y no respondes.
Como espero tu respuesta
Sin saber lo que piensas
con las esperanzas de un día poderte ver
Y tú alma conocer.
Batalla con tu corazón,
razonas con tú mente
Y con tú boca lo declaras
que no puedes enamorarte de mí
Porque no aceptas que yo no soy mujer de juegos
Que soy muy directa con mis palabras
Mi corazón es un libro abierto
refleja mi honestidad
Que no te escondo nada,
soy firme con lo que siento
Y tengo mi propia entidad
no me avergüenzo de amarte
Y ni tampoco de declarar
que soy una mujer enamorada
Y tú eres el hombre mas afortunado
en que mis ojos se fijaron
Y vieron una gracia en ti
Ningún hombre ha podido
desviar mi mirada fuera de ti
Considérate honrado
de tener una mujer como yo,
Porque mi valor es grande
Y si no te has dado cuenta
éstas muy equivocado.
Pues mujer buena es muy difícil encontrar,
Recuerda: que la belleza es vana hermosura,
Pero un corazón justo vale más
Mujer de corazón humilde y que teme a Dios
¡Esa hallara gracia delante de los ojos de Dios!

Te Espero

Mi amor con deseos enloquecidos te espero
Deseo con pasión ardiente amarte para siempre
Tenerte entre mis brazos, sentirte junto a mí
Tú calor y energía calentando mi aura
Con tú esencia apasionante dejando me el universo
Apreciándote cada segundo, minuto y hora que pasa
Juntos amándonos en nuestro propio paraíso.
Dejando en el espacio rastros de ilusiones
Para que otros amantes desean tener lo nuestros.
Dejar nuestra estrella fingida en el universo
Y toda la noche brille con nuestro reflejo
Para que toda persona que nunca ha encontrado su
Verdadero amor pueda hacer su pedido
En memoria de nuestro encuentro
Esperanza fingida encuentre su inesperado amor.

Ven conmigo

Ven que contigo quiero comenzar
Un sueño que no acabará.

No, temas al tiempo que la luz del cielo
No se apagará

Voy a ensañarte lo hermoso que es el amor
Cada piedra será una flor
Cantaremos a un nuevo sol.

Ya no hay sendas que puedas volver atrás
La alegría de un mundo mejor tendrás

Ven levanta tus ojos
A los cielos rojos del amanecer

Hoy en el mundo entero
Una primera flor puede florecer

Deja que el viento se encienda con su rumor
Pinta el mundo con tú color
Y cantemos a un nuevo sol

Los dos sonriendo; toma mi mano y sigue adelante
Gloria y fiesta es la vida cuando hay amor.

Hasta Cuando Piensa Seguir Así...

Hasta cuando piensas seguir así...así lejos de mi lado
Hasta cuando piensas pretender que no me necesitas
Y que yo no te anheló

Eres como un niño mimado
Hasta cuando piensas que el tiempo ha de esperar
Y que yo te seguiré esperando

Hasta cuando juras ser fuerte
E ignorarme por puro capricho

Hasta cuando piensas que solo tú eres necesario
Y no hay otras razones de tenerme a tu lado

Hasta cuando piensas que el roció de la mañana
Solo cae en tu ventana
Hasta cuando piensas que el sol sale temprano
Para solo aclarecer tu camino

Hasta cuando piensas que las estrellas brillan
Tan solo para tu admiración

Y que el mundo gira sólo a tu lado
Hasta cuando piensas que nunca envejecerás

Y una mano cariñosa desearás
Cuando ya no puedas más caminar
Sin hombro para afincar
Y tu cuerpo soportar
Cuando ya no puedas ver
Y mis manos desearás para guiar tu camino
Cuando ya no puedas oír
Y solo mi voz dulce te hará feliz
Cuando solo mi calor como un niño
Mimado necesitarás

Hasta cuando tú opinas que no te sentirás solo
Cuando se supone que el tiempo parará
Y nunca has de ponerte viejo

Hasta cuando seguirás pensando así
Pues el tiempo no ha de parar por ti
¿Hasta cuando piensa seguir así? ¿Hasta cuando?

Tu

Tu solo fuiste un amigo inesperado que no supo apreciar
El cariño de una amiga
Quien nunca te ha de olvidar
Los tiempos mejores de mi vida
Los viví contigo
Las mejores memorias aunque aún tan cortas
Son los mejores recuerdos que quedan en mi alma

Tu no supiste darte cuenta que yo era la mujer para ti
Pero me fuí lejos por que ya no pude esperar
Solo para darte el tiempo
Para pensar
Así ver tu vida y analizar
Pero aun así no tuviste cuenta de mí
Fui solo otra mujer quien cayó
En la red del pescador sin remordimientos
Tú muy fácil te olvidastes de mí
Ni una sola palabra sabia de un hombre inteligente
Ni una excusa planificada
Ni una mentira falsificada
Ni una ilusión extraviada
Solo el silencio de tu miedo
Lo he sentido hasta en los huesos
Tu cobardía es solo tu fingir que esta en lo cierto
Que no me necesitas y que yo soy muy simple para ti
Una estrella que brilla sin fingir
Una luz en tu obscuridad esa soy yo
Una rosa despojada
Una lágrima en tus ojos
El beso de tu Nina
Aún te traen mis recuerdos

Pues un ser limpio y bueno
Difícil es de olvidar
Tú quizás te crees que nada perdiste
Pero fíjate mi amigo que al perderme a mí
Lo has perdido todo
Pues yo pude ser
Todo para ti

Mi Despedida

Tú eres el hombre que yo siempre estaba esperando
Como un sueño, en otoño, las hojas caen y vuelan con el viento
Así ha sido tú presencia en mi vida, inesperado llegastes
Y con el viento fuerte del invierno partistes lejos aún no regresara
Dejastes solo tú sombra y recuerdos de tú voz a mi despertar
Nunca supe lo que fue tenerte entre mis brazos y amarte con pasión
Ni vi. El alba de la mañana
Ni vi. Las estrellas a tú lado
O la plena noche de luna llena
Tú partida dejará un vació en mi corazón con el alma entera sufrir tu
decisión
Y aprenderé a olvidarte despacio y con determinación
Podré olvidar de que a mí llegó mi real y primer amor
Pero el a mi no me encontró
Adiós....con estás líneas entierro mi amor por ti...

Final, Despedida, el Fin, se Termino

I
Hemos llegado al final de nuestro cuento.
Tú y yo ya no somos los protagonistas
Hemos llegado al final de una historia.
La cual no se realizó

Fue cortada en la mitad por tu orgullo y pretensión
Eres tan cabeciduro que no sabes entregarte al amor
Tu supuesta agenda es más importante que preservar un amor
Que débil eres por darte por vencido, por puro capricho
Y no saber como salvar el amor de una amiga la cual te amó

Despedida no tuvimos, pues tú no sabes
Como confrontar cuando hay conflictos en el amor
Para ti es más importante tu trabajo, tus amigos, tus intereses
Y tu orgullo de vivir como un hombre soltero
Es una meta cual tú no quieres cambiar
Porque esperas ser libre hasta la muerte
Eres esclavo de los placeres de tu mente y tu cuerpo
Para ti el amor no existe pues nunca lo has aceptado
Y nunca lo has experimentado

Todo para ti es conveniente y disponible
Tú lo reemplazas de momento y cuando te cansas buscas algo nuevo
No es verdadero lo que tanto buscas
Es solo un buen tiempo por el instante
Nada permanente en tu vida tú permites
Ni siquiera el cariño de una amiga

Mucho miedo tienes que conozca verdaderamente quien eres
Que pena que te conocí
Como ninguna había podido
Y te conocí más allá del corazón
Contemplé tu ser y te acepté
Vi lo bueno de tu alma

Eras el hombre de mis sueños
Pero tú con tus caprichos te engañas
Debates con tu mente
Razonas con tu corazón
Que no puedes ser una realidad este amor
Tú vives en una fantasía
La cual no te deja ver la vida en lo real

II
Eres como un niño consentido, egoísta,
Y malcriado que solo piensa en sus deseos
Lo que vez en el espejo es superficial
Tu orgullo es tan grande que solo te deja pensar en tu "Yo"
Te dices a ti mismo que solo "Yo" me necesito y yo soy único en "mi"
mundo
Mi espacio no lo comparto con nadie no se compartir
Vives una fantasía de caprichos y engaños
A nadie sabes decir yo te extendí mi mano

Vives por tus amigos como si algún día
Estarían disponibles para estar a tu lado cuando solo te sientas
Cuando ya no puedas más darle la mano
Espera solo su compañía vives sus fantasías
Y así llegarás a viejo y algún día te preguntarán por quien lloras
Y no sabrás como decirle "por la mujer que debí amar" cuando tuve la
oportunidad
Y ahora solo quede y sin ese cariño completo que ella me dio
Me quiso como nunca me habían amado más yo a ella la he despreciado
En soledad me he quedado

Mírate bien mi amigo
Fíjate bien en lo que haces
Examínate bien físicamente y aprende a ver por los ojos espirituales
Deja que tu corazón aprenda amar
Deja que tu mente acepte el cariño y el amor de una mujer de compresión
Amigo mío quisiera enseñarte amar, quisiera hacerte ver lo bueno que es
mi ser
Quisiera que me aceptes y me puedas ver con los ojos del alma
Deseo que luches por nuestro amor y no me dejes perder
Amigo mío quisiera darte un pedazo de mi alma
Para que puedas tener la capacidad de un amor honesto.

Pero que triste es que nuestra historia ha llegado ya al fin
Ya la conclusión está comenzando hacer escrita en el papel

Que pena que nuestro libro se ha quedado en mitad
La historia larga que hubo de ser ya no será
Se ha vuelto sólo un pasaje de cuentos de hada que nunca se cumplió
Como todo buen escritor el libreto sigue en mi despacho

III

Encima de mi mesa quedan sólo los retazos y fragmentos de papel
La historia fue destrozada como lo fue mi corazón
En una esquina en mi recamara aun queda un pedacito de tu recuerdos
Esperando ser dispensado y al fin terminado

Con el fuego en el fogón
Con las cenizas y polvorín se escapan todas las memorias de un amor
quien espero, observo; ha si como sube el humo en el viento

Se ha terminado mis esperanzas
Y anhelos de seguir esta historia
El fín ya llegó…

Spanish Expressions
Part II Debates de mi Alma

Lo que mi Alma Desea

Mi alma desea un compañero que me acepté
Que me comprenda y no me avergüenze
Que me entienda y no me ignore
Que pase sus mejores tiempos conmigo
No se aleje pero que se acerque

Compañero tu eres mi anheló
Pasar los mejores tiempos contigo eso espero
Discutir, hablar y comparar cual sujetó y aventura
Caminar y comparar los horizontes
Viajar por todo el mundo y conocer las diferentes culturas
Navegar el océano, y conocer otros mares
Compatir la belleza de las naturalezas

Tú mi compañero te esperaré, para compatir contigo;
Mis mejores sueños, mis mejores ideas, mis mejores anhelos
Tú mi alma conocerás y unidos estaremos
Amigo mío mi alma te desea
Decídete y no esperes más
Que los tiempos pasán muy rápido
Ahora es nuestro tiempo, no mañana

Lo que mi Alma desea es que me aprecies
Como una piedra preciosa
Que me conozcas como la persona interesante que soy
Que me preguntes lo que no sabes, y lo que hay de saber
Comunicarte conmigo y no esperar que la tensión crezca
Acéptame y no me rechaces
Entiéndeme y no me confundas
Atiéndeme no me preguntes
Escúchame y hacedme caso
Comprensión y se paciente
Y una compañera tendrás para siempre
Una amiga sincera
Una esposa fiel
Una mujer especial
Eso es lo que yo seré para ti

Lo que mi alma desea es tenerte junto a mí

Un Amigo O Amiga

Un amigo o amiga saber dar de si mismo sin rencillas
Está dispuesto en cada momento
Extender tu mano cuando la necesites
Te escucha aunque no te entienda
Está de acuerdo aunque por dentro lo debate
Trata todo lo posible para estar a tú lado
Te habla y platicas de muchas cosas aunque no tengas sentido
Llorar contigo y reír contigo
Desea lo mejor para ti
Te ayuda a ver lo mejor en ti
Un amigo o amiga en días malos y buenos siempre desea estar a tu lado
No te abandonas cuando ocurre el primer desengaño
Te perdona y no guarda rencor
Te espera con paciencia hasta que pase la tormenta
Cuando viene la calma te recibe como si nada ha pasado
Un amigo no es solo cuando te conviene
Un amigo es para siempre
Yo soy tu amiga y lo seré para siempre
Porque una amiga no se dará por vencida

Querido Amigo Mío

Solo espero que te encuentres bien. Yo por lo menos lo estoy
Te tengo que decir que siempre me haces falta igual que ayer.
No esperaba tú desprecio, ni tampoco tú alejamiento.
No se porque te he extrañado tanto y ni tampoco entiendo la razón
Por cual mi corazón se siente triste
Fui sincera, no te mentí
Siempre te he dicho la verdad de mí
No pretendo y ni te engaño
Pues yo no se jugar esos juegos del alma
Ni tampoco se como atraer un amante
Pues yo no tengo tanta experiencia en esa área.
Soy orgullosa de que soy así tímida y confidencial en mis costumbres
No soy como otras que tú has conocido y no te pintaré una imagen que
no es
Pues yo soy, "Yo" una mujer firme y sincera en mis palabras

Yo no esperaba que esto me sucediera a mí, yo no quería enamorarme de
ti
Yo solo quise ser tu mejor amiga y aceptar tu vida tal cómo es
Pero no me culpes por que te amo, no te alejes por tú miedo
Pues fue mi corazón quien cayó, y en las redes de tú alma se enamoro
Mi mente me falló no supo ser fuerte y también te amó
Y que te digo de mí ser pues él primero nos conoció
Que yo y tú podemos ser una unión equilibrada
Pues los dos somos seres que nos necesitamos
Y un reconocimiento perfecto entre tú y yo

Piensas bien de lo que te vas a perder
No seas terco y deja que tú mente y corazón
Tome ya la decisión de amarme
Pues yo me merezco lo mejor
Soy mujer buena, y fiel
Si he sabido sufrir en esta vida pero no por lo merecido
Fui victima de la vida y de muchas malas decisiones en el amor
No tengo cosas materiales ni tampoco fama al exterior
Pero llevo en mí un tesoro en mi corazón
Pues lo único que te ofrezco es mi amor y comprensión
Seré fiel hasta la muerte y te amaré para siempre

Si te atreves no te alejes
Deja que mi ser y el tuyo nos encuentren
Y cumplir lo que se comenzó y compartir nuestra vida con amor
Ya tu verás lo que pasará los dos felices y en paz

La Esperanza y Confianza

Esperanza es tener fe en que algún día volverá
Y como un viento invernar regresaras
Esperanzas como sale el sol en la mañana con su resplandor
Y alumbra mi ventana al despertar
Esperanzas como cuando sale la luna alumbrando con su luminosidad
Y con las estrellas brillante fulgor decoran el cielo con ardor
Esperanzas como el roció de la mañana que acaricia las flores
A su despertar y besa la grama con sus caricias
Esperanzas como cuando los pajaritos cantan por de mañana
Y anuncian un nuevo día en su rutina
Esperanzas como el mar con su potencia las olas vienen y van
Y siempre llega a la orilla del mar
Esperanza como una flor que sale por primera vez
Y su perfume deja al por doquier
Esperanzas como un bebé toma su primer respiro
Y llora por primera vez
Asi es las esperanzas que yo tengo en que un día tú has de regresar
Y a mis brazos has de llegar

Con la confianza que yo tengo en mi Dios y mis creencias de fe
Tengo la esperanza que mi amor volverá
Y esta vez no te escaparás

Pues ya hasido mucho tiempo
Que te has alejado y es tiempo de regresar
Confianza te doy con las esperanzas
De cambiar tu manera de pensar

Recuerda que un amor verdadero no es lícito dejar perder
Por puro capricho de tu orgullo

Y por no saber reconocer que con esperanza
Se recobra todo lo perdido y lo que nunca ha habido
Pues es el comienzo de algo nuevo y que dura por toda la eternidad
Así es la esperanza que tengo en ti y en mi

Perdón un Dialogo

Un dialogo en secreto pues no hay contacto entre tu y yo ni tan si quiera
por teléfono
Pero mi alma aún lejos siente que tu ser me llama y aún deseas mi
amistad
Y mi dialogo comienza así...
Perdóname si te estoy molestando, pero me he sentido conmovida en
saber como estás
Hoy hacen semanas y de ti ya no se nada.
Mi Corazón me dice que algo te ha pasado
Perdóname si me preocupo de tu vida,
Pues eres mi amigo y todavía a mi me importa tu existencia.

Por favor, no me desprecies, por puro capricho, escúchame que nada mas
deseo
¡Saber como tú estas amigo! Tú sabes que yo no te logro olvidar
Y al saber que mi Corazón me decid igual
Yo siento que estas sufriendo una dificultad muy grande
Y se me rompe el alma cuando siento tu dolor.
Y aunque esté lejos de mi yo siempre estoy cerca de ti,
Pues mi ser siempre está contigo desde que entraste en mi Corazón.

Perdóname amigo mío, ya sé que te has decido y no quieres saber que yo
continuo
Me entristece saber como te sientes, pues yo no te hecho nada para
causarte sufrir
Tu desengaño viene de otras caídas, y yo nada tengo que ver de eso.

Creerme, amigo mío, que me entregué en carne vivo, te di mi ser, mi
Corazón
Y también mis pensamientos. Fuí honesta, y pura cuando me tuviste
entre tus brazos
Y al fin en mi alma encontré una parte de mi ser, la cual yo nunca había
tenido en mi vida
Yo justamente lo único que soy culpable es de amarte
Yo no lo esperaba, yo no lo demandaba

Pero tú llegaste y me robaste parte de mi alma
Fuiste tú el culpable amigo mío

Amigo mío, por favor no me desprecies pues te amo con toda mi alma
Y nunca te dejare de amar
Y aunque lejos estés, todavía sufro por tu desprecio,
Y cuando pienso en ti lagrimas caen como una lluvia en verano
No se lo que me pasa en esto días, pero siento que estas sufriendo
grandemente
Y quisiera con toda humildad, que supieras que yo también sufro contigo

Pues inevitablemente siento lo que tú sientes,
Y cuando aun tu triste estas, mi Corazón aun lo siente
Quisiera hacerte feliz, pero no puedo
Pues tú conmigo ya no quiere nada
Amigo mío, tuvistes un ser bueno entre tu brazos

Quien pudo ver mas allá del pasado
Te ame y es mi único pecado
Y he quedado con un fragmento de tu alma en mi costado
Y aunque no creas, lo que yo siento es real

II
A dios le pido que te cuide y te guié en tu vida
Pues mis consejos y reclamos ya no escuchas
Y solo debates aún cuando me tienes a mí en permanencia
Y finjas que no me necesitas, que yo ya no existo para ti

Que tristeza saber que estas perturbado y mi consuelo menosprecias
Cuando yo te conozco también y se que me necesitas
Aunque no lo quieras admitir, mi alma lo percibe
Amigo mío, tu no sabes las faltas que me haces
Estoy segura que mi cariño tú aun lo quisieras

Pues tú sabes mejor que yo que así es como te sientes
Y aunque lo niegas, mi corazón es testigo
Como hacerte comprender que tú y yo no somos una equivocación
Que tú y yo somos dos personas muy distintas
Pero nos citamos equivalentemente
Tú eres el polo negativo
Y yo tu positivo pues los dos nos completamos el uno al otro
Igualado

Estos días son tan difíciles para mí, saber que ya de mi no quieres nada
Yo siguiere siendo fiel a ti, aunque los años me lleguen sin pararse
Amigo mío tu fuistes mi otra mitad, el ser que yo esperaba
En mi soledad le pido a Dios que te guarde en tus días

Como paloma blanca en días de invierno, cuando aun la nieve cubre mi
ventana,
Abrir mi ventana y te he dejado ir
Eres libre, pues yo no puedo hacerte amarme
Y libres estás como una paloma blanca
Sobrevuela, alto en los cielos sigue tu camino
Sin sosiegos y yo aun anheló que algún día te determines
Deseo con mi alma que vuelvas algún día temprano

Y si un día te acuerdas el camino a mí corazón
Y ha de retroceder a mi disposición
Con una mente dispuesta,
Y un Corazón abiertamente
Y un ser libertado
Entrarás otra vez en mi ventana
Con una hoja de laurel en tu pico
Y una lágrima en tus ojos cristalinos
Por lo tanto adiós amigo mío
Que Dios favorezca nuestro destino

Amor de Viejo

Cuando creas que nadie querrá oír tú voz
Llámame...
Cuando sientas deseos de verme
Buscame...
Cuando creas tener sentimientos de Amor
Siénteme
Por que yo soy de tú vía cruz
El monte calvario

La ultima cuenta que habrá en tú rosario
La ultima hoja de tu calendario
La ultima oveja de tu rebanó
La "Z" del abecedario
Soy tu futuro, presente, y otoño
Soy el diciembre de todos tu años

Juntos estaremos hasta que lleguen
Los años de envejecimiento
Y dicha será estar a tú lado
Y los dos juntos tomados de las manos
Y recordaremos los tiempos felices del pasado
Que hermoso será tener la dicha
Y ventaja de amarte para siempre
Hasta que el ultimo suspiro salga de tús labios
Cuando la muerte será la única razón
De estar apartado
Y aún así esperaré
Volver otra vez
Estar a tú lado
Pues en el cielo
Seremos hermanos
Amor de viejos por largos años

Cobarde

Hola como te encuentras, ya hacen días que ya no sé de ti
Ningún adiós, ni hasta luego ni tan siquiera nos vemos…
Nuestra despedida fue muy triste y entiendo que no lo esperaba

Pero me cansé de jugar juegos, y es por eso que me tuvé que ir…
Nunca dijiste si me quieres y nunca respondistes a mi cariño
Fuiste muy duro conmigo y tu orgullo te llevará a la perdición

Pues dejastes que tu carácter te dictara lo que podría ser entre los dos
Me rechazastes y me abandonastes. Ni siquiera me dijistes adiós…

Ya no importa pues sigo sola, en mi soledad me he dado cuenta que no
vales la pena dejar que un hombre como tú rompa mi corazón…Y he
crecido espiritualmente y entiendo que yo valgo mucho para cual otro
hombre que me sepa valorar.

Fuistes cobarde, y un mentiroso pues todavía tu mismo te niegas que
también me amabas. Me da mucha pena que no tuvistes fuerza internas
para atreverte a pelear por nuestro destino.

Que tristeza me da saber que esa fue la razón que me perdistes y no
seguistes luchando por nuestro amor. Yo soy una mujer que te quiso con
todo el corazón y nunca supistes apreciar el cariño que te rendí

Y aun con los abrazos abiertos siempre te acepte. Nunca dudé que eras
un hombre bueno. Ni tampoco me avergüenzo de quererte.

Delante de Dios he declarado que siempre te amaré. Y a Diós le pido que
algún día tú también llegues amar como yo, y en esos días te recordarás
de esa mujer tan simple que te amó.

Y en la vida se repite la misma historia de un amor traicionero.

Como Entender

A veces tenemos que perder alguien en la vida
Para poder saberle apreciar

A veces cuando creemos estar libre
Es cuando aún mas atados estamos

A veces cuando más fuerte nos sentimos
Es cuando aún mas débil nos hallamos

A veces cuando queremos con más anhelos
Es cuando mas difícil es procurar
A veces cuando mas tranquilos nos sentimos
Es cuando mas inquietos estamos

A veces cuando más quiero la paz
Es cuando mas viene la Guerra

A veces cuando trato de entender
Es cuando mas confusa estoy

Como entender….
Cuando a veces no veo la realidad de la vida
Cuando la soledad me cubre
Y no me deja respirar
La sombra de él aún veo
En la obscuridad

Como entender…
Que cuando un amor se va
Ya no hay mas duda
Que el nunca ha de regresar
Como entender que no me quiso….

En la arena del mar

En la, arena del mar
Quedo dictada la historia
De dos amigos
Que pelearon por no enamorase
Pues el orgullo fue más fuerte
Y ahí en el mar

Pisadas quedaron
La tuya y la mía tomada de la mano
El sol crujiente quemaba mi espalda
La nubes reflejaban claridad esperza
Un día temprano en la mañana
A las cinco nos levantamos
Para nuestra gira en el mar

El olor de café
Al abrir los ojos
Incitaba nuestros ánimos
Recuerdo que tu almuerzo
Muy feliz te preparaba
Con una sonrisa en mis labios
Te ofrecía tu taza de café
Te ayudaba a preparar
Tu nevera con agua
Y juntos llevamos
Las varas de pescar
Todas anillada en un esquina lista para salir

Salíamos contentos
Sin ninguna pruebas
O preocupación
Solo anhelando
La vista del mar cuando saliera el sol
El barco despacio salía de la bahía
Y con fuerzas rápida
Rocíar las olas del mar

La brisas del mar
Acariciaba mi cabello
El aire limpio y puro
Respiraba
No nos hacia falta nada
La felicidad y tranquilidad
Existían como la naturaleza
Y allí en el mar
Mi ser se atrevió a conocerte
Me enamoré sin razón ninguna
Sin ningún esfuerzo de tu parte
Pues lo que existía era más fuerte
Que tú y yo
Mas cierto que los peces en el mar
Fue lo que encontré al ver tu ser

Una seguridad de que tú eres mi pareja
La cual tanto tiempo yo esperaba
Esa otra mitad
Que existía
Y yo nunca lo sabía

Pues fuistes tú el hombre
Que conmovió mis entrañas
Y de lo más profundo del mar
Clavaste el anzuelo
Y te amé desde aquel momento
Y quedé confundida porque
Tú no abriste tu corazón
Sino excusas pensastes
Por tu miedo y orgullo

Tú quizás te mientes a ti mismo
Y tratas de tu mismo convencerte
Que no, así no fue
Solo fuistes una compañera del momento
Pero que mentira y decepción
Cual pretensión llevas acabo
Tratando tan fuerte de engañar tu mente y corazón
Pero la lucha que llevas

Por tu orgullo
Has clavado una lanza en mi corazón
Así desechada he quedado

Pero recuerda que la historia aún no ha terminado
Pues en la arena del mar
Quedó fingida
La historia
De dos amigos
Que pelearon por no enamorarse
Pero uno de ellos cayó.
Y en la arena lo escribió

Perdí todo el valor de mujer por ti

Perdí todo el valor de mujer por ti
Pobre de mi por lo que quise ver en ti
En el comienzo existía cariño y atención
Pero después cambiastes como de la noche a la mañana
¿Y nunca supe por que?
Silencio extendido hasta el universo
Sordo, mudo extrañado
Ya ni sabe
Que excusa darme

Tus sentimientos no los sabes expresar
Lo bueno de tu ser lo escondes
Pretensión de lo humano
Fuistes un actor pero de lo más malo
Pues no supistes tu libreto y no me convencistes
Que no me quisistes

Fue una acción menospreciada
Dado al tiempo de lo inesperado
Como intelectual pensastes egoístamente
Como hombre fuistes cobarde
Como humano no aceptastes mi amor
Como confundido espíritu lleva la cruz
De tus pasares
Y sin aún dejar los sufrimientos en el antepasado
Esperar triste un milagro
Que llene tu vació en tu alma
El roto que hay en tu corazón
No se remienda con aguja
Sino con amor y aceptación
De que alguien te quiso con toda su alma

En ti vi lo que nunca quise imaginar ver
Pues tu ser transparente pode ver
Vi tus fallas, delitos, y dolor
Y aun así
Con gracia te ame
No tuve miedo

Porque sentí que yo era la cura
Para tu débil vivir
Yo era la sonrisa en tus labios
Fui la risa a tono alto
Caricias y sinceridad te brindé
Te amé como ninguna te amado
Y fui la diferencia en tu vida
Aunque no lo creas
El sentido común de razón
La expresión de nuevo día
La claridad en tu ventana
El dulce de mi cariño
Aún te hace falta
Y así como yo
Lloras lagrimas amargas
De tu corazón
y aun tu ser sentía el dolor
De la pérdida de nuestro amor

Anhelas como yo
Nuestro calor
Sentirte a mí lado
Y acariciar tu cabello negro como azabache
Tus ojos café cual brillaban
Cuando me miraban
El resplandor de la alegría que sentía a mi lado

Yo también igual que tu
Te extraño
Mi vida no es lo mismo
Cuando compartíamos juntos
Ya no se como dejar de pensar en ti
Pues el valor de mujer lo perdí
Cuando me enamore de ti

Dejé todo aun lado
Y me entregué de alma y cuerpo
Aún te sigo amando
Te di lo mejor de mí
Y un trozo de mi ser te has llevado

Y con está antología
Te expreso mi sentir
En el transcurso del tiempo
Te he amado más que ayer
Y con esperanza milagrosa
Te seguiré esperando
Fiel y pura
Guardándome
Para cuando te vuelva a ver

En La vida

En La vida pasan cosas muy difíciles de entender
Aunque tratamos y tratamos no podemos comprender
Difíciles momentos
Difíciles tiempos
Lagrimas corren
Derramando dolor
Pues lo que pasó nos ha desquilibrado
Las memorias quedan pero duelen los recuerdos
La nostalgia de lo que pudo ser
Y no llegó el momento

El transcurso de los tiempos muy largo fue
Quedé como una hoja seca en el camino
Y en el camino de larga espera
Imaginando los escenarios
De los momentos felices
Entre tú
Y
Yo

Cuando todo parecía color de rosas
No se oye ni la bulla entre los
círculos de gente
Solo el silencio de tú y yo
Me fui
Pero muy lejos para dejarte pensar
Esperé que los recuerdos te persiguieran al igual
Pues a mi no se me pierde ni uno
Los datos pasan en mi mente
Como plumas en el aire
Recuerdos entre tú y yo

Que lindo fue lo que fuimos
Que bello fue nuestro encuentro
Tu mirada y la mía fijada directamente
No perdiste ni una chispa
Pues mis ojos alumbran como estrella en el cielo
Tus caricias fueron reales

Y tu mano aun la siento en mi piel
El calor entre tú y yo
Química hecha en los cielos
Cariño, ternura
Amor de primera vista
Fuimos tú y yo

Con un bolígrafo y papel

Con un bolígrafo y papel así me desahogo
De todos mis pesares
Con las letras que escribo expreso
Mi quejido
Con cada estrofa sentirás
Mi lamento
Los versos de los más bellos
Los escribo contigo en mi pensamiento

Queden grabados todos los datos
En declamación
Cuando y siempre declaren
Nuestro amor
Esta dedicación
Es un recuerdo para tí
Que en mis mejores años
Te encontré a ti

Que desventura cuando
No apareció
La sombra tuya en mi espejo
Porque te fuistes lejos
Y fueron esfumados los recuerdos
De la silueta la cual no recobro ver
Por la ventana
Y muy lejos pero lejos
Te veo
Pero cuando quiero alcanzarte
Es cuando mas lejos te desvías
Apartándote de mí tu sombra
Pero en mis sueños
Como fantasma espeluznante
Apareces claro y resplandeciente

Pero que triste nunca veo una sonrisa en tus labios
Solo tú mirada tristemente
Cabizbajo
Seriamente y cuidadoso

Tu mirada hacia abajo
Pues tu ser triste
No puede mirarme a los ojos

Quisiera abrazarte fuertemente
Y quizás así te olvides de tu dolor
Con besos hacer borrar todo
Lo que te ha hecho sufrir
Con mi amor hacerte ver
Lo dulce de vivir
Que cuando se ama de verdad todo es posible
Todo lo malo se va
Todo lo bueno llega
Se esparce en el firmamento una estrella
Dedicada para nuestro comienzo

Que en la vida las cosas difíciles de tener valen la pena
Que el que espera pacientemente no se lo lleva la corriente
Milagrosamente cosas bellas llegan
Y
Aunque
Tú no lo creas
Yo espero pacientemente
Segura de mi misma
Orgullosa de amarte
Confiando siempre que cuando se ama
Lo reclamo en alta voz
Para que todo el mundo lo sepa
Porque cuando se ama de vera
No hay miedo
Ni rencor
Solo
Esperanza
Y fé
De algún día volverte a ver

Spanish Expressions
Part III Reflejos Y Sueños

Quien Soy Yo?

¿Quien soy yo? Y lo que un día fui
Soy una mujer de integridad
Fui yo una tonta enamorada
Lo que fui y lo que ahora soy
Es totalmente distinta
¿No soy aquella quien no pensó?
ahora soy pensativa con el tiempo
Lo analizo todo en el momento
No se me pierde nada
Lo recobro todo
No se me pasa nada
Sin que yo no lo vea primero
Astuta como una serpiente
Pero mansa como una paloma
Como lo dice la Biblia
Así me considero yo
Ya los tiempos de engaño y desengaño no existen
En mi vida solo existe lo positivo
No lo negativo
No hay espacio
Pues no acepto mentiras, decepciones y engaños
La verdad más franca que puedas expresar
Mírame a los ojos no tengas miedo
Dime lo que sientes, piensas y deseas
Yo no te atrasaré
Sino te empujaré a seguir tus sueños
Yo no seré un estorbo sino una guía
Yo no seré distracción si no un empuje
Píensalo bien
Decídete ya
No sigas ya perdiendo el tiempo
Apresúrate
Porque sino me pierdes
Estoy cansada de esperar
Soy fiel a ti
Y ni así
Me estimas
Te amo como el aire que respiro

Quisiera pasar los mejores momentos contigo
¿Pero donde estas?
Silencio, miedo y en obscuridad
Está envuelto en un debate de si o no
El miedo no te deja agarrar lo que es bueno
Silencio nocturno
Habla ya
Se escucha tu suspiro en el aire
Que el tiempo corto ya está
Oscuridad porque la luz de tu ser se oscureces
La tristeza se refleja en tus ojos
Y al parecer aparentas muy bien
Pero tú ser lleno de angustia y sufrimiento
Lo veo en tu reflejo
Pero queda la luz mía cual te alumbra
Un camino resplandeciente
El cielo claro
Las nubes despejadas
El sol resplandeciente
En el camino yo te espero
Con los brazos abiertos
Ven recíbeme ya
Que anhelo estar en tus brazos

A Veces

A veces cuando siento ganas de rendirme y alejarme de ti
Pienso esos momentos bellos que hemos pasados
Y siento una alegría en mi Corazón por tenerte a mi lado
Cuando estamos juntos es como si nuestro mundo
Es sólo para los dos sentimos una paz y tranquilidad
Que nunca habíamos encontrado en otra persona
Mas tú y yo lo hemos realizado

Tú me has enseñado amar sin condición
Te amo sin restricciones
Te respecto tal como eres
Admiro tu carácter
Y deseo estar a tu lado para siempre
A veces pienso que bello será compartir contigo
Mi día y noche, mi mañana y mi futuro
Saber que está cerca de mi a todo tiempo
Y que te sientes feliz con mi atención
Deseo conversaciones, discusiones y dialogo inteligente contigo
Deseo irme a pescar los dos juntos
Y ver la belleza del mar desde el amanecer
Hasta que baje el sol otra vez
Mi amor es verdadero
Y puro
No deseo nada más que tenerte a mi lado
Pasarte la mano en tu castaño cabello
Y verte sonreír en el momento
Saber que te encuentras feliz
Con mi firmeza
Deseo mas que nunca compartir tú día conmigo
A veces pienso como te anhelo
Y mi corazón se pone triste
Y lagrimas corren de mis ojos en saber
Que no te encuentras aquí, a mi lado

Un Paisaje en un cuadro

Un paisaje en un cuadro pintado en mis memorias
Con pintura de aceite y
Colores claros
Que brillan como espejo
Y aun veo tu reflejo

Así como en el comienzo de mi vida
Dijo el pintor pintaré un paisaje de una vida inocente
De felices días en el pasado cuando en mi niñez
No había dolor de ninguna clase
Cuando las lagrimas solo resbalaban
Cuando me golpeaba o me caía
Cuando los días eran tan largos que ni del tiempo me daba conocimiento
Cuando la noche era tan larga que aun esperaba que llegara la mañana

El pintor cambió sus colores claros a colores de pasteles
Pues mi juventud llegó y no esperó
Gozar en juegos e intereses
Ir a la escuela ¡aprender de la vida ya llegue!
No sabia de peleas ni sabia de enemistad
Solo pensaba en amigos y amigas para con quien jugar con rapidez
Mi radio escuchaba para oír canciones de amor
Pues esos eran mis pasatiempos
Juventud llegó pero no se quedo

El pintor sigue pintando y colores obscuros utilizó
Colores rojos, y amarillos y verdes y marrones
Pues entré en mi años de adulto
Con versatilidad y carisma
Creyendo que el tiempo no cambiaría
Y que en la vida todo igual se quedaría
Adulta llegué hacer y me case como todo el mundo
Pero de mis ojos lagrimas fluían pero no de alegría

Nunca supe de tristeza antes
Pero ahora lloraba como un niño
Los años llegaron y mi inocencia robó
El paisaje del pintor ya no se ve igual que ayer

Un paisaje obscuro y triste al resplandor
No es la misma pintura que usa el creador
Ya no usa pintura fina y clara en color

Los años han llegados y el paisaje más abandonado
Colores triste y gris
Mucha sombras en el pasado
De los acontecimientos que el pintor aún se acuerda en reminiscencias
De lo bello que fue el comienzo
De esperanzas fingidas
De un amor que nunca volvió
Y la oración de una amiga
Que sola quedó
El pintor ha agregado con su vejez una estrella en la esquina
Esperando con fe algún día ver su amigo
Y así pasan los años
Y aun le quedan fuerzas para pintar

El pintor seguirá pintando su panorama en clamor
Que grite a todas fuerzas con su alma y corazón
Para que todo que admire este cuadro
Pueda apreciar la señal pintada en su panorama
Para todo aquel que no ha encontrado
Su verdadero amor
El recuerdo de sus años en un retrato ha quedado
Y con la espera han llegado los años
Y en un almacén se encuentra su cuadro
En una pared para que toda vista pueda ver
Para cual apueste lo más alto
Pues antiguo y valioso es su cuadro
Que en la espera de los anos ha quedado
Esperando aprecio y estimación

El Destino

Muchos dicen que solo uno individualmente hace su destino
Muchos dicen que lo que más uno quiere es lo que no se puede
Que el camino corto no es mejor que la vereda ancha

Que todo lo que se hace difícil en la vida vale la pena
Quien dijo que la felicidad sólo tu eres el dueño
Quien sabe si la persona que tú más desprecias es la que verdaderamente
te ama
Quien sabe si la compañía que tienes no es la que te conviene

Fíjate bien lo que buscas en la vida con tanta ansiedad y que no te traerá
felicidad
Fíjate bien que lo que tu te confabulas eso mismo en la vida será tu fruto
Fíjate bien que el mundo es redondo y gira alrededor del sol y todo
vuelve a su lugar a su tiempo
Fíjate bien lo que haces con tu vida, que la mentira, traición
Y maldad no te expongan en un torbellino de obscuridad
No dejes que en la obscuridad te pierdas por tus avaricias y fantasía

¿Que vale perder tu ser por una hora de placer?
¿Que vale perder tu integridad por un poco de cariño?
¿Que vale perder la luz de tu ser por puro capricho?
¿Que vale perder a Dios por un engaño del enemigo?

Que triste es revivir lo que haz hecho en tu vida
Que triste será verte en tu mismo desprecio
Que triste saber que en tu alma no hay amor
Que triste saber que no escuchas la voz de Dios

Como explicarte lo bonito que es tener la gracia de Dios en tu vida
Como explicarte la grandeza que hace Dios en mi vida
Como poder hacerte ver los milagros que Dios hace si tienes fe
Como dejarte saber que tu sufrimientos y los míos mi Jesús los llevó en
la cruz un día
¿Como hacerte ver que por su sacrificio hoy tienes el libre albedrío de
tomar la decisión de servirle o no?
Como hacerte comprender que algún día clamarás a Dios
Y con tus manos directas a los cielos Misericordia gimieras
Perdón Señor, perdóname, dame tan siquiera tu paz hazme ver

A Dios le pido que no se te haga tarde,
Y que encuentres la única felicidad en la vida que es en él
Que solo Dios puede cambiar tu vida
Y llenar el vació en tu corazón

El gozo más grande que nunca haz experimentado en Cristo lo hallaras
A Dios le pido que te bendiga y toque tu corazón
Y con los oídos del alma puedas escuchar asumir el plan más perfecto de tu vida
Lo cual el un día lo trazó, esperándote con paciencia te espero
Amigo mío no rehúses escuchar este clamor
Del alma mía a Dios le pido que te haga ver la realidad
Que nunca es tarde para cumplir las metas que verdaderamente hace una diferencia en nuestras vidas

¿Que puedes llevarte contigo si te mueres?
Pues nada, todo se queda para quien lo herede
Ni la fama, ni dinero, ni amigos, ni amores, ni mujeres, ni placeres
Todo se queda aquí en la tierra
¿Que vale extenderte hasta lo ultimo para tener la admiraciones de los hombres?
Que vale si tu mente y corazón se te pierde por tus resentimientos
Y perdonar no puedes por tu orgullo
Misericordia a Dios le pido, que tenga misericordia de ti.

Los Caminos de la Vida

La vida trae muchas sendas diferentes
¿Por cual cojo?
¿Y cual me beneficia mejor?
Es la pregunta la cual todo individuo se hace
Y trata de responderse por si mismo

Entiendo que todo pasa por un propósito y razón.
Así se ha dicho hasta en canción
Prevenir o interrumpir o quizás no repetir
Pues nuestra capacidad determina a donde iremos
Y con quien andaremos en nuestra larga jornada
Pues mira bien quien te acompaña
Y quien es que te esta señalando dirección
¿Para donde ir y con quien andar?

Fíjate bien que la dirección tuya no es la misma de él o ella
Tú mapa solo Dios lo sabe
Y él solo puede ser tu guía
Pues él ha formado el firmamento y su planes
Cambia nuestro destino sin nosotros saberlo
Nadie sabe lo que le espera
Ni tampoco su propósito en su vida

¿No te enoje? Porque adonde quieres ir se te hace tan difícil
Puedes ser que Dios está velando tús pasos y ya sabe lo que te espera
Hay veces que nos trata de dar señales
¡Por ahí no! ¡No entres! ¡No sigas! o ¡desvíate de inmediato!
Por cabecidura/o seguimos al paso lento

Como tortugas lentamente caminos en perezas
Esperamos llegar a un sitio y ser recompensados
Pues tarde llegamos y mucho tiempo perdimos
Seguimos fijados con cosas de este mundo
Y la tortuga de nuestra vida no llega a su meta del destino
¡Nos creemos que esa es! Pero que equivocado
MUCHO TIEMPO SE HA PERDIDO

¡Hay que pena! Sigues buscando y quizás un nuevo plano te encuentres
Y perdido sigues buscando por las montañas
Y al llegar a la cima ya no vez nada más
Ciego buscas y sin guía adonde vas hacia abajo
Y de repente te encuentras en un valle calle boca abajo

Y una pequeña puerta estrecha vez a lo lejos y un anciano
Y el anciano te dice:
"Hay veces que nos desviamos y por otras sendas anchas caminamos"
Por valles profundos, y llanos
Amplia senda es nuestro motivo
Muchas distracciones en el camino
Pues el panorama es bello y nos absorbe
Y nuestra vista se enfoca en cosas vanas y materiales
Y andamos perdidos comos pobres desamparados
Sin esperanza y sin fe en el mañana
Solo existiendo por el momento
Como si eso es lo que Dios ha determinado

Pues nuestra meta está en cosas dispensable, aturdidas
La cual nos llevaran a ningún lado
Sólo a la perdición y la oscuridad
Y solitos andamos por una senda tan grande
Soledad, tristeza es nuestra única compañera
Y no hay nadie que extienda sus manos
Y ni tampoco un buen consejo por la cual te diga:
"oye hermano cuidado adonde andas y quien llevas a tú lado"

Recuerda que a veces es mejor pasar por sendas estrechas
Aunque sufras y te sientas cobijado
Dios siempre estará a tú lado
Y hay veces que necesitamos pasar por larga sendas
Para que aprendamos una fuerte lección en el la Vereda.
Y quizás así recapacitamos y nos volvemos a su lado
Dios es paciente y nos espera con sus brazos abiertos
En la entrada y como ovejita perdida nos llama
Y con su amor y ternura nos invoca a la senda que el nos a ofrecido
Y nos guía con fe, esperanza y amor
Pues estas son las preferibles guías que nos llevan a la

Reverencia y nos alumbran la ruta
Cuando la obscuridad llegue
Y como faro de luz en el horizonte la luz del sol sale todos los días
Y Dios nos recuerda de sus grandezas pues el cielo es testigo
Mirando hacia arriba la hermosura de su naturaleza
Vemos que grande es nuestro guiador
Y el firmamento de su gloria
Pues tenemos que estar agradecidos
Y decirle si señor guíame que aquí estoy
Solo tú sabes la vía

Soñar

Ayer soñé
Un sueño maravilloso
Te vi en el mar
Pescando
Con vara en mano
Esperando
Un sombrero en tu cabeza
Y sólo te vi pescando
Una silla cerca de ti
Un cubo para tu pesca
Una sola esperanza anhelas

Y el hombre pescando en su afición
En su hábito de pescador
vació a la derecha
Su pareja lejos
No esta a su lado
Su amiga
Encantada de pescar con el
Ni invitada
En su retiro al mar
Su silueta en su lado derecho existe
Su sombra
Su sonrisa
Su mirada
Ojos verdes claros como esmeraldas
Te miran
Existe mi presencia a tu lado

Anhelando aun el día
Cuando juntos otra vez
Dos valientes pescadores
En su gira en el mar
Buscando especie diferente
Bajo el sol caliente
El agua pura y clara
Reflejo del amor
La cual este pescador

Pudo tener cerca de el
Pero el anzuelo removió
Y otro estilo recobro
Alcanzar pescar algo exótico
La cual no podrá disfrutar
Pues la marea
En su ritmo

Exigió
Un cambio de pesca
El mar crujiente
Las olas fuertes
El viento en su furor
El bote sube y baja
Con las olas en sincronización

El tiempo cambia
Y aun el sol salio otra vez
Las nubes negras
Ya se fueron
La claridad se esparce en el cielo
Te veo de lejos
En el mar luchando
Con tu vara en tu mano
El viento te espanta tu sombrero
Pero no cedes de tu mano tu vara
Y con fuerzas sigues luchando
Para alcanzar esta pesca
Extraña
No te recuerdas que un día
Tu amiga tuvo a tu lado
Y tu fiel ayudante
Dándote todo los anzuelos, varas y
Línea de pescar
Por favor pásame agua
Que tengo sed
Aun se escucha en mis oídos
Tú amiga fiel una botella a tu mano
Ya la puesto
Pero que triste es sentirse como si ya ella no existe

Ella en la orilla del mar espera alcanzar verte regresar
Una sombra desde lejos
Un señor con un sombrero
Un bote va pero muy lejos
La ruta sur no fue su coordinación
Al norte el cambio
Ni dijo adiós
Pues no era mi pescador
Solo un señor con un sombrero
El pescador compañero
Ya se retiró del mar
El mar atlántico,
Y también el golfo medio
además el mar de los recuerdos
Pues solo era un sueño

Adiós al Año Viejo

Adiós al año viejo, te llevas mis recuerdos
En una nube solitaria te llevas mis pesares
Pues con tu partida arrancas mis sentimientos
Aquel quien robo mi corazón te lo llevas lejos
Ya lo que hubo, ya no es
Lo que era, ya no será
Lo que compartimos ya no existe
Y tu voz ya no la recuerdo
Tú mirada ya está lejos
Una sombra en un espejo

Quisiera tocarte pero no alcanzo
Quisiera amarte pero no me dejas
Quisiera hablarte pero como silencioso sosiego te apartas
Yo ya no existo para ti, me has olvidado como el año pasado
No recuerdas nuestros momentos
No me deseas como yo quisiera
En un mundo diferente te encuentras
¡Hay de mi! que te amé
¡Pues ahora como una tonta quedé!
Y los recuerdos de los años
Con el año viejo han sido despedidos

Como quisiera volverte a ver
Como quisiera amarte otras vez
Como si fuera la primera vez
Tenerte entre mis brazos
Y suavemente acariciar tú piel
Abrazarte y no dejarte ir
Vivir lo nuestro una vez más
Y comenzar de nuevo en el año nuevo

Adiós, año viejo te llevas mis mejores recuerdos
De un amor que no me supo amar
Un hombre me ha utilizado mi corazón
Y con su partida se ha extraviado
Y ya no tiene memoria
A si como se olvida el Año Viejo...

165

Yo fui una vez ignorante

Yo fui una vez ignorante pero ya no lo soy
Creí en todo el mundo
Pero ya no creo ni en mi misma
creí en el amor
Ahora en la soledad
Yo una vez creí que todo el mundo decía la verdad
Ahora entiendo que yo solo era la ignorante
Pues no sabia de engaño
Y ni tampoco de mentiras
Pues en mi mente no entraba ese concepto
Y no era fácil de entender

Creía con todo el Corazón que todo el mundo era bueno
Pero ahora he caído en cuentas
Que hay mucha gente mala en el mundo
Yo nunca creí en el odio
Pues nunca lo había sentido
Yo nunca creía en la decepción
Porque nunca lo había sentido
Pero ahora que lo experimentado
Y con dolor lo he aceptado

No fue fácil mi descubrimiento
No lo pude aceptar
Que aún en mi ignorancia
No quería admitir la realidad
Pensé que todo el mundo
Veía el mundo de colores como lo veían mis ojos
Lo bello y distinto que yo veía
No era lo mismo que otros decían
Que en la vida uno no puede ser tan bueno
Porque abusan de lo humano
Con grandes burlas y despecho te hacen sentir tan inexperto
Porque creíste en una persona
Que sólo sabe decir mentiras
Que nunca ha sabido amar
Pues el concepto nunca lo ha conocido
Ahora digo yo ignorante es el que no sabe amar

Pues en su ignorancia le cogió miedo al cariño
Corriendo como un animal asustado
Se ha escondido en su incapacidad

Mi Oración

Con lágrimas y llantos de lo más profundo de mi alma
Hoy señor a ti clamo
Como una llamada de emergencia hasta los cielos
Así clama señor mi alma
Como el Salmo 42 que dice así
"Como el ciervo clama por las corrientes de las aguas
Así clama o Dios el alma mía "
Escucha mi clamor Dios todopoderoso
Recibe mi oración como ofrenda preciosa

Mi ser turbado está dentro de mí y aún me faltan las fuerzas
A veces tengo ganas de rendirme
Pero sigo, sigo insistiendo
Que mi oración llegue hasta tu trono
Y responda a mi clamor

Dame las fuerzas para seguirte señor pues no es fácil este camino
He cambiado por completo no soy la misma mujer de antes
Tome mi decisión de seguir tus caminos pero todo se me ha sido difícil
Me han abandonado hasta mi familia y amigos
Ya nadie comparte conmigo
Soy una extraña en mi tierra vieja
Extranjera en mi propia ciudad
Pues ya no soy la misma persona de antes
Soy distinta y es la pura verdad
Todo aquel que me llegué a ver
Se da de cuenta en mi cambio espiritual
Que a mi vida ha llegado la paz
Y no hay necesidad de otras cosas
Si no el amor de mi Dios
Ese amor incondicional que ningún hombre me pudo dar
Ya los tiempos míos han pasado
Y a mi edad he determinado que lo único
Que verdaderamente vale la pena
Es mi relación con Dios, Señor escucha mi plegaria
Con toda mi alma me despojo de todos mis sufrimientos
Se mi consuelo en estos momentos
Mi oración como ofrenda te ofrezco

Creo en Dios

Creo en Dios, los cielos cuentan sus grandezas
El firmamento, es testigo
La obra de sus manos
Evidencias en todos lados
Los océanos un mundo desconocido,
Profundo, delicado y aun ningún humano
A explorado el fundo de los océanos
especies desconocidas
Valles y llanos no nombrados
explicar el universo
misterioso y místico en lo cierto
En gigantescas calculaciones, ningún hombre a podido
Confirmar lo que ha existido
No se encuentran soluciones ni tampoco factores científicos
De lo que hay más allá de la eternidad
busquen, y busquen jamás encontraran
Pues el inmenso universo solo Dios lo controlara

Dispersos secretos y misterios descubrirlos buscan más y más
Pero aun sin suficientes evidencias
Para los hombres aceptar
una figura grande y poderosa
responsable de lo que los hombres buscan
Creo que en ese inmenso firmamento de los cielos
Existe el verbo que era, que fue, que es, y será
El Alpha y la Omega
El Principio y el fin

Que lo creó, lo fundo, lo nombro, y lo salvo
Para que todo en que el crea no se pierda más tenga vida eterna
Quien es el hombre si no puede aceptar
Lo que Dios hizo con sus manos en su amor
Y aun en el mundo siguen dudando, escarneciendo, buscando,
examinando, y explicando
Lo que Dios tan simple puso a su disposición
Y que nunca podrán comprobar su hipótesis
Porque solo Dios es la conclusión, solución y la respuesta
Para todo lo que el hombre busca en su curiosidad
¡Ya frente a sus ojos existía la verdad!

Quisiera Tocar el Manto del Maestro

Quisiera tocar el manto del maestro
Tan solo tocar su vestido
Para que todas mis penas y dolores desaparezcan
Mi tristeza y mi llanto puedan ser calmados
Con su misericordia Dios me perdone
Y como el lodo del alfarero el me haga de nuevo
Que molde mi espíritu y mi vida sea nueva

Mi humilde oración le pidió que la aceptara
Que toda lágrima mía vea como perfume
Que mi llanto suba hasta los cielos
Y Dios en su misericordia me escuche
Dios perdona todos mis pecados
Por favor borra todos mis errores

En tu gracia te pido que yo pueda tener
Una oportunidad en mi vida de ser bendecida
Gracias te doy Dios que no me abandonastes
Que cuando mas sola me he sentido tu estabas conmigo
Mis cargas tu llevastes por mí Jesucristo
Y toda lágrima que de mis ojos fluyeron tú la has secado Señor,
Quisiera tocar el manto del Maestro
Tan solo tocar tu vestido
Que con mi fe mi vida sea un milagro
Que con mis esperanzas tú me uses para animar a otros
Con tu Espíritu Santo mi vida sea guiada para que otros puedan ser salvo
Mi testimonio Señor es solo para tu gloria y honra
Que por tus llagas Señor curastes mis heridas
Por tu sacrificio me salvastes
Tu misericordia Señor me ha dado fe, esperanza y animó
Para seguir luchando en esta jornada
Me enseñastes Dios a ser paciente
A dejar todo asunto en tu manos
Que sea tus voluntad mi Dios
Que mi vida sea un milagro

Ever Been In Love?
Part I The Beginning

True Friendship

As the wind blows fiercely on a Winter morning,
Briskly making its way against my windowpane,
So is the story of our beginning and our end....
Quickly and earnestly was your call to friendship;
Cold and fiercely was how you ended it.
Hear the wind hissing and the sounds of a lover's good-bye.

With the night cold and dark, hear the tears dropping by
On the cold floor of my lonely and desolate bedroom,
See the shadow of the man who was to be my best friend.
Through the window I see the stars and wish upon them
That I may forget that friend who caused my anguish,
And with every tear that I shed I swear that I will never trust again.
For how can you say you know how to love
When you can't even keep me as a friend?
No apologies, no mistakes, no error, and no sense of what happened to
us.
No farewells, no good-byes, and not even a note to say thanks for being
my friend.
It's not a **right** and it's not a **privilege.**
Friendship is earned, valued, and held onto until year's end....
So how can you say you are ready to love
When you have skipped the most important step?
For in life you need to keep at least one true friend
Who doesn't ask, demand, or want anything in return,
But waits patiently for your response.

Your friendship, that is all; what more can you doubt?
I heard an old wise man say, "What is life without a true friend?"
So value those you have, hold on to them with you all your heart.
Don't let go, because in life there comes a time
When we might need the soothing words that only this friend can
provide.
And in my eyes, with every tear are broken promises, broken dreams,
And a broken heart—I am left without the soothing sound of your voice
to heal.
With every tear that I must shed I promise you this: I will always be you
True and only best friend.

I won't forget you, because I will always carry you inside my heart
And in my prayers you always will be,
For it will be the only way that your soul will be close to mine.
So as long as I live I will always wonder about you.
I know that with every face that comes close to looking like you,
I know that once again I will experience the pain
Of losing my best friend....

One Day I Met a Gentleman

One day I met a gentleman
With a serious demise
Who sorrow I could see and feel
By looking into his eyes
His pain
And hurt
I felt
I saw
I experienced
No telling how
Or why
What
When
Explanations all failed
I tried to reason within me
I try not to remember what I saw
But what I felt in my mind and heart
Was as real
As a bird that flies
Singing a new song
Telling me
It's him
You know him
You feel him
You sense him
You hope for him
You have faith in him
You trust in him
You see all the good that is in him
For real love can surpass the soul
See the growth that ought to happen
Allow it to grow like the example of "a bud into a rose"
Has anyone ever told you?
I love you for you!
Accept your eccentricity
You just have to accept mine
Expressiveness: that's me

So what are you waiting for?
Your lady awaits you
With faith in her heart
With hope in her mind
That the love I have for you
Will never die
Silently I wait for my gentleman
Whom I now understand so well….

<u>Beginning of Us</u>

In the beginning we started with an e-mail
and then proceeded to a phone call
First time in my life that I had tried
an unconventional method to chat with somebody
I was scared and, being the shy person that I am, I felt awkward
I thought that maybe this is crazy, and maybe we both were!
But for some reason every time I looked at your picture
I felt that I knew you
It was a strange feeling, but I lost all fear
and connected with you anyway

I felt that you were the one individual that I needed to connect with
Somehow I trusted you and I felt secure to do so
An indescribable feeling, to get to know you deeply
An energy which pushed to want to know more about you
The most strangest thing was that I already knew you
for I had seen you in a dream
as if I was getting reacquainted with an old friend
to share times together once more
Your silhouette has been with me ever since I was a child
You were that stranger that I had always seen in my dreams
that man I knew to be my soul mate
for your face I knew a long time ago
As strange and weird as it sounds
I knew you

You see, somehow in life we both took many wrong directions
Our paths were always distorted
You never had found what you were looking for
and I never met what I was searching for
But somehow something kept us apart
We both have gone through many rough experiences in life
I felt your pain, I saw what you went through
and I still cannot explain how.
Amidst your suffering your heart has hardened
given up on finding the beautiful soul you've been waiting for
the one that was right in front of your eyes

You overlooked, blinded by so many distractions
and overcome with pleasure-seeking attitude
You failed to see that I was right in front of you
You see, we're not a mistake
and I am positive of it
because you and I were meant to be
Somehow we both made wrong decisions in life
You have been seeking, searching, and waiting
for your soul mate
And I have been also waiting alongside of you
Both were living in the same area but failed to meet
Why?
Because many negative forces have kept us apart
not allowing this process to happen
You see, we are to unite spiritually
This is what our souls lack
You are strongly diverted into a life of superficiality
that you no longer believe
You do not see with the light of your soul
for your eyes are blinded
your heart is hardened
Earth and sky fighting a tornado
separating us

For we are not on the same spiritual level
and somehow I feel that you have given in to worldly sins.
I cannot reach out any longer
I cannot make you see what I see
and I definitely cannot make you feel what I feel
I believe that God has used me to tell you a message of hope
I do not doubt it, because at the time I did
I was not equipped to say the things I said
or to write to you those messages from God
Because in all humbleness I was not there spiritually
Having been saved, I now comprehend the complexity of it

You and I are two strong bolts of energy
that God wants to bring together for a purpose
I am the calm of the storm arising in your spirit
I am the peaceful vessel that extends all her love to you
the natural sweetness that comes from within
the heart that shines and lets others see

For I live my life in the open
I do not hide my experiences and pain
I share with others openly
With an honest heart I can conquer all
You are to me that intelligent man with which I can keep conversation
going and never get bored
I am the listening ear to hear all your fears and troubles
to comfort you and guide you
How else can you explain the comfort level we had
that peacefulness in our souls when we shared together special moments?

Not only did He assign you to me
and made me for you
but He also had an amazing plan for us to accomplish
and to do His work together
We are meant to work together on a task so amazing
We both have been chosen to be ambassadors from God
The concept hard to explain
You might even disbelieve
But I can only speak what the Lord has told me
I have never reached out to anyone with such an assurance
let alone spoken to them about God
With you I felt the urge and confirmation
that I had to
I did what God instructed me to do
I did my part

If you do not listen to His message
It will be between Him and you
Jesus is the one we have to give account to
Not humans
Remember, pleasure, women, drugs, and immorality are here for the
moment
But what happens if you become ill or suffer a life mishap?
Do you think that you will be able to seek pleasure?
Do you think that you will be able to be with women
except for the medications you will be given?
Will your friends be around to help you out?
Will your lover stay?

Will your colleagues help you with your financial debts?
Be realistic; we are living in a very superficial and materialistic world
Temporarily they will connect
but it will become too intense for them to stay
Live and learn from your mistake
Don't continue following the same cycle
substituting friends for the real family
substituting love with a physical attraction
substituting spirituality with people's admiration
Think hard, my friend
Search your heart instead of ideas
Be real and learn to be yourself instead
Don't lose yourself and your culture to assimilate another's view
To become what they are
is not what God has set you out to be
For He knows the plans
He has for you
plans to prosper you
to give you a future
to seek Him with all your heart (Jeremiah 29:11 NIV Bible)

For this is what is important
If you died, what would you take with you?
Nothing?
So why forfeit your soul to the devil
to experience worldly treasures?
Why not invest in your soul instead?
Think of the reasons He allowed us to meet
A message of hope I shared with you
in the beginning of us
with all my heart and soul
Rethink, evaluate, and search
For what is truly important in life
is your spiritual salvation...!

Today I Sent You a Message

As I sit near the beach watching the waves
slam against the rocks with torrid force, I look at the ocean.
The waves slam high and mighty as they pass by.
Blue with its frothy foam they come and go
with perfect unison, as if they are making music.
What are they playing?
They play the music of love and hope
that my soul mate will return one day.
The wind strongly forces itself against my face
with such a strong blow that it leaves me breathless.
My hair flowing all around in the air,
I feel my cheeks getting the cold caresses of the wind
as if kisses were blowing into it.
I feel in touch with nature and loved by it.
In appreciation I gently look at the waves,
softly wishing that they could send a message
with their rhythm to you wherever you are.

"Please hear me calling you.... I need you to hear me saying I miss you.
I wish you could hear me now and feel what I am feeling.
Open your heart and hear me calling. I know you can hear it.
If you do please do not ignore me.
I know you are as confused as I am."

I could be that soul mate you have been looking for,
but your fear doesn't let you accept it!
I will be patient and I will wait.
I will wait until your heart opens up to receive me.
As the waves come and go,
silently I will wait for the day that you come to claim my heart....

When We First Met

When I first met you, your eyes met mine, I chilled with fright,
and you opened up some senses that were long lost.
You made me realize how easy it can be to fall in love.
Looking in your eyes, I see many secrets.
They remind me of how I used to be.
When you speak, my loneliness and heartache is forgotten. When you
admire me, your eyes are like the ocean in a storm, great waves that
caress me and surrounded my soul.
So I write about you as if I have shared a life span of loving and caring
for you.
But it's no secret I just met you!
And my dreams can't just be. For I know that there might be someone
else loving you
and the reality is that there is no one here with me.
Alone I wait until we meet again....

The Kiss

I remember as if it was just yesterday
When you first looked into my eyes
There was nothing between us then
A passion, a warmth, a positive attraction which pulled us close
Looking into each other's eyes, experiencing no fear
The light in my eyes shone like bright stars
Leading you to look into my soul and see beyond
As I looked into your eyes, I felt your pain
And saw beyond what anyone else had dared to see
I felt a strong energy, which pulled us so close

The kiss just happened as we searched into each other's souls
I still do not have the words to describe the feeling of our first kiss
It was the most amazing feeling I have ever experienced
I felt loved, I felt like I had known you before
It felt so natural; I felt so much love that day
The kiss was quick but so intense
That I felt it last very long in our own world
My heart and yours connected some how
Your mind and mine met each other that day
Your soul and mine reacquainted with each other

Remember how much love I felt in my heart for you that day?
I felt that I had been yours before—no telling how it could have been
All I knew was that I was completely yours that day
No feelings of regret, no shame, no inhibitions
I felt like this is how love is supposed to feel
This is how being intimate with someone you love should feel
So natural, so comfortable, and so loving

Our intimacy was so special—I never had experience it before
It felt as if I had been waiting for so long to meet my soul mate
Once connected to the warmth and energy within each other's soul
So deep the feeling I was experiencing in my heart and mind
It was a timely synchronization of two souls in search of each other
Finally finding the part that was missing
So intense, overflowing with a natural energy, confirming
That yes, this is real and it is how it could be

You were so content inside, for I felt it deep in your heart
Your eyes, they told me how much you wanted me
An experience like two married people in their honeymoon phase
It was amazing, for every time we came together intimately
It always felt as if it was the first time
We talked for hours and hours, did not feel the need for sleep
For we were so interested in each other that nothing else seemed to
matter
It was beautiful, it was real, and it was our fate for us to meet
I often wish I could go back in time, be loved like that very day
Relive the sweetness of our encounter
Relive the warmth and love of our first kiss
How much I miss you and wish that you could come back to me again
Pull me in your arms and kiss me so deep like that very day of our first
kiss

Why? Why? He's Got Me Feeling Butterflies ...

I am so far above the ground
I can make believe
I reach the skies.
Feel his love is my only wish,
Hope for his love in return is my fate.
Dream of him is my constant reflection.
I live a daydream that he is my lover,
Dream to narrate the next scene that plays in my heart and mind.
My heart feels the strong longing to be the one he finds true love with.
My body craves for the warmth touch of this dark
And handsome stranger I've met.
I ask myself how this could be,
Wishing to be wrapped in his arms,
Feeling the passion within hearts as this love becomes one.
This sweet and pure love waits for the day
That this man could fix his eyes upon me
And only me,
The woman who truly loves him, no doubts, no fear, and forever.

Rendezvous

You came along at a time when I felt my world
had been shattered by painful experiences.
My existence had just lost its appearance and solitude had entrapped my
body;
I thought definitely I had disappeared from existing.
I had lost all the will power to believe in love or that it would ever find
me.
But when I met you and you said, "Hello," for the first time,
our eyes met in unison and a spark of life escaped from you and touched
my heart.
I felt like I had known you all my life, like a lost friend had come back to
life.
A childhood memory began to surface and the face of the shadow of the
man I always dreamed about became reality somehow.
Here I was in front of the man that I have waited for all my life.
Your silhouette has been in my mind all of the days of my existence
and I never knew that you really existed.
Then suddenly a desire to make love to you enveloped my body
like a soft wind in the middle of Spring.
Then before I realized it, there we were so vulnerable to desire.
A desire, which swept us closer, your lips touching mine, my body
quivering in ecstasy.
Your masculine hands softly caressed my body with such care and
affection.
You fondled my breast with such sensitivity and passion.
You finally entrusted your body to mine;
a flame began burning inside, and then we became one.
Suddenly, I felt like I belonged to you before, now and forever yours.
A rendezvous which was meant to happen, me and you are no mistake.
Somewhere in time I have found you….

It Was Just a Dream

Last night I dreamed I was walking on the beach with you.
Your arms around me, we walked the shore; the sand felt cold and rough.
The night was still, and near the beginning, the sky was dark and the
stars shone bright, the wind gently blowing, sending chills down my
spine.
The sea gently gave its waves like sweet caresses as it reached the shore,
it's spume slowly reaching the edge of the shore and disappearing
swiftly.
The moonlight reflecting in your eyes, you handed me a rose and said,
"I want you." Without hesitation I looked at you and gently kissed your
lips;
you responded with such excitement, you startled me.
The last thing I could remember was the smell of the sweet roses that
filled the air in the warmth of my bedroom. It must have been a dream,
but did I wake up in your arms?

Listen to Your Heart

Listen to your heart; don't debate
Clear your mind; you will discover
The answer you've been looking for
Don't be so hard-headed
Thinking you know all the answers
Thinking that your intellectuality
Will dictate your happiness
And be your companion for the rest of your life

Remember, like Einstein's theory of relativity
You and I equal square
A perfect solution to a complex problem
I solved the equation that was missing in your life
And you have solved mine
Therefore, we are in perfect unison
Can't you see we understand each other perfectly?
For we are meant to be
You and I are soul mates
Why doubt such a complete equation?
Our chemistry equation is simple: **YOU + ME =**
Understanding, patience and partnership, love
Results in a balanced equation with peace and tranquility
What we both desire we find within each other's arms
The chaos in our lives tries to keep us apart
But our energy is so strong that it pulls us together
And even when we try to keep away from each other
There is a catalyst of overflowing love that pulls our energy together
So don't fight it
Let it flow
Let it grow
Let it become whole
We will become one
So listen to your heart and your brain will lead
Meet me where I am and a perfect love will follow

Ever Been In Love?
Part II The Soul Connection

Answers From the Heart

How do I know I love you? Well, it's an easy answer for me.
I grew to love you and that was my downfall; never thought it could happen to me!
I'm mature enough to know that it's real,
for I have had enough experiences in my life to know the difference.
You said it was a mistake, after we met;
it is the cowardly way of not accepting that something good can happen between us.
But your unrealistic expectations of what love can be,
your confusing way of thinking, tells you no, it is not "she."
Your philosophy of living life without restrictions,
intimacy: it's too intimidating for you.
Getting to know someone deeply is too threatening for you.
It is easy for you to close out all of your emotions,
numb them, and make believe you don't have any.
It is your self-defense mechanism to avoid getting close to me.
Your vision of what a real women can be is distorted.
A pretty face, nicely shaped, no content, just beauty is what you seek.
A young girl to make you feel young at heart, for you are fighting hard to stop time.
No visions of maturity in your mind, you see, for life to you is just about having fun.
No seriousness about the realities of what a real relationship is made up of?
You shun me like a disease, thinking you are just better than me.
Screen yourself with the scanner of life, and tell me if you think that's right.
The way you analyzed, scrutinized, and evaluated me,
it's just a narcissistic point of view.
The only woman you let in your life is someone who thinks of pleasure all of the time,
the superficiality of not accepting life's responsibilities,
or seeing that aging is a process that eventually everyone will go through.
But happy is he that can accept it with grace
and see how lovely everything around them really is:
wisdom, understanding, and caring traits that matter in any relationship.
Kind words come from the heart, not from a script that's played.

Loving kindness is not a ritual, it's daily practice, even with your own enemies.
A pure heart and a clean mind is not a disability.
It's an honor to have known someone who values and upholds life,
who does not destroy in a rage of anger because of selfish desires of the flesh.
I fought and fought to keep myself clean, and no wonder I value me.
I know that it's easy to blame others, life, and the pain of living,
give up and say, "I am angry at the world for my own mistakes."

However, I found that there is a valuable lesson to learn from errors, mistakes, and bad choices,
humbling our souls to know that God was always and is the only way to find joy in our hearts.
Spiritual enlightenment we all seem to be looking for,
watch out: there are many wrong ways we can try to realize it.
Perhaps what you seek so deeply has been waiting for you in front of your face,
searching and searching: different color hair, different color eyes,
different shape of body, and different view of life.
The more you seek the harder the search becomes,
because eventually no one will ever meet the prize.
You will get tired of trying to fit the Cinderella shoe on the many different women in your life.
Indefinitely, you're seeking in the wrong places and times,
not paying attention to the matters of the heart.
But who am I to state these things? Why should it matter to me? A secret
I will tell you is: not fame, fortune, or money matters!
For when you die you won't be able to take it,
but someone's unconditional love will last a lifetime.
Don't pay no mind to your past mistakes.
Accept you as you are; don't need to change.
Your silly habits, nitpicks, and eccentric ways,
I know them well; don't need to hide them, I accept them.
Your silliness and ways about you, I learned to missed them.
I can't seem to forget your craziness, and I enjoyed every minute of it.
An intelligent man who acts like a fool, for he is to proud to accept the woman of his dreams,
pridefulness because of what his friends might say, you let others make decisions for you instead.
I please others thinking I am pleasing myself.

I want their acceptance in order to have their friendship,
agree that I must let go of my own cultural values and way of being
so others can enjoy the new me. I was not happy being me
so I decided to become somebody else's gig.
So what's wrong with loving someone? What's wrong if he does not love
you back?
What happens when the world revolves around and he soon finds out
that the world is round and everything revolves around the sun,
taking us to the same place we started?
Experiencing the same, he failed to acknowledge
the pain and heartache you will feel.
For no one is immune to the rejection of someone we love.
Just wait a while, your turn will come.
Fall in love so deeply and true
and with your feelings she will play you like a tune,
the melody of pain and disdain.
Then you will remember me, but it will not be in vain....

If Only Your Heart Knew ...

I hope that you can see what love really is....
I never knew until now that love is a decision you make
to accept another human being as he/or she is....
To make a decision to love someone
you have to be willing to incorporate it into action...,
meaning that you have to love the
individual even when they have hurt us....
Accept them, forgive them, and keep loving them.
You see, I never understood before what "LOVE" was.
I had it confused with how that individual provided for me financially,
because he did not even know the meaning as well.
I forgave myself for my mistakes;
I forgave that individual as well,
for in his heart he tried the only way he knew to give love....

Now my life has changed, my character as well.
I am a strong woman who knows what she deserves.
I never thought you could love someone
even if they don't get anything in return.
I love this special person who's stolen my heart and mind.
I love him in secret, for he does not know that
I patiently wait in silence
and pray for the love of my life to come my way.
I sometimes question, does he even deserve it?
He does not send anything my way.
But I pray and ask God for answers,
and He tells me that he needs that love I have for him,
and the only way to fight for his love is to pray for him.
Why? I ask God. His answers are always there.
For in his heart he has never found someone who has loved him for him.
So profound is my love that I often feel his pain:
I sense and see so many things in his life that I can't explain.
One day I heard that if you love with all your heart, mind, and soul,
God will answer your prayers.
For I am not selfish and because I love this man so deeply,
all I want for him is to be happy.

I am not worried that he does not know,
or that he is not physically here with me.
For in my heart and soul I am always there with him.
My prayers are that this man can realize how fortunate he really is
that God has called him into His plans
and he needs to follow Him instead.
I pray so hard, with my soul open for God to hear,
that I'd rather he get saved than be with me in place of
For I know the plans God has for him
and I'd rather that he finds his way,
and that he learns the real meaning of life
by the love I have in my heart for him.

I often think to myself if it was years back,
I would not have wasted my time even praying for this man.
I would have thought, he doesn't deserve it; he is a very selfish man.
It's a mystery to me and hard to explain
but I know that he and I are not a mistake.
He doubts because it comes easy to him.
He is trapped in fear and confusion
because I do not meet the superficial plans.
But I, however, meet God's spiritual plan.
I never once intended to love this man,
but I have been taught a hard lesson in life.
Good things come to those who wait....

My only wish is that he finds God and doesn't let any distractions come
his way,
for it's been too long, the struggles he has faced,
the heartache and all the pain.
He struggles daily with two extremes, one of evil and one of good,
for God knows there is no in between.
He lets himself be dragged from one edge to the other,
and when he realizes the mistake that he has made
his mind and soul is weary, for he is in too much pain.
He knows very well the decision he has made;
he understands that pleasure is only temporary,
but his mind struggles with some

powerful inner conflicts that lead his heart astray.
The struggle that you face, I also feel your pain,
for I believe that I am here to let you know
that with love you can conquer it all....
For I know that I will not give up on you,
no matter how distant you've become.
Because you need my love, heart, and mind to help you win this fight.
And one day, whether you are here with me or not,
you will have won the final score,
for in your heart, mind, and soul you will be set free.
God will be fighting for you instead
and holding your hand as you walk along the shores of life.
For I believe in miracles.
Let me tell you that I don't give up easily,
and this is one I will not give up on.
For I know that my God can overcome it all.

At this moment he might not even understand it
and even refuse to listen to God's call.
But one day you will come across a very difficult situation,
and in a moment of desperation when all else fails,
and the only hope he will have would be to call on the Lord,
let us hope and pray that then it will not be too late.
For He has been calling you since birth
and the reason that his soul is restless is
because he has refused to listen
and he constantly ignores Him at all cost
This is the very reason his mind struggles in distress,
for he needs something to make him forget
and has dubbed down the voices in his head,
which constantly are telling him,
"My son, I've been waiting; when are you coming home?
I love you in spite of all.
Give me a chance
and I will make your pain all go away."

Please give your heart to the Lord
and let him guide you.
You will be sure to find your way.
For He knows the best route and path to take.
Remember, he knows you very well.

Why I Love This Man

I cannot understand why I love this man.
Does he even deserve it?
I tried very hard not to let him know how I feel.
For I am also afraid of being mistreated.
When I realized that I love this man it was already too late!
My heart and mind have been given away.
I know it was not a crush .
I've been there, done that.

I know it was not an infatuation; I am not a child anymore.
I am a grown, mature woman who knows and understands what it is to
love.
I am secure enough to know that it is the real thing.
I had always wanted to experience true love
Then I met him.
I realized that I own my heart and mind,
the fact that he has not yet done anything to deserve my love.
However, I know that I cannot give up on him.
I love him and even if he is not with me,
this is real and I miss him more each day,

as if part of me has died,
as if part of me is missing.
It is such an intense action that I cannot explain in mere words.
For I battle each day to forget him.
I struggle within myself to make believe that I do not love him.
However, I only end up fooling my heart but not my mind and myself.
I'd sacrifice my heart and soul to have never known this experience.
I am at a point in my life that I settle in my ways.
I am confident of what I feel and what I want.
I accept his decisions
but I miss him like hell.
However, I understand that sometimes in life
you find the one but the one does not find you.
It is all about acceptance, talking it out, and reaching an agreement to
become partners;
to challenge each other to see that in spite of our differences
we have many similarities.
This can enable us to work together as a team!

I am woman who has reached the point in life that if it did not work out,
I am not going for someone else!
I am tired of sharing myself.
I am tired of giving but not receiving.
I am tired of being true but not having the honesty rewarded.
I am tired of being so naturally loving.
I give of me because I am open, down to earth.

I am me; why could he not see that of me?
Why he did not see the beauty in my heart?
The light and love that shines?

I thank God every day for meeting you.
I have been blessed to find the other part of me.
My friend, love of my life, I will never love anyone else.
I am mature to know that it is real.
I do not have the time or energy to try anymore,
for there are many liars out there.
I know who I am.
I am not afraid to stay by myself.

I am happy with me.
I feel secure with myself to know that it is okay to be me.
No need to search for something I have already found.
I found and lost it too quickly.
I do not want to put myself through any more pain.
I have decided that there are other things I could do with my life
than wait for a man to love me back.
As long as God is with me and I have His grace around me
I have nothing to fear.
Life is too precious.
I will seek other things in life instead.
Finish my goals in life,

travel, and help others in need,
Give of myself to others who will honestly appreciate it.
I think to myself what have I done? Why did he run away?
Afraid of the challenge of accepting the real thing,
afraid that for the first time there is someone who would not let him
down,

not give up on him no matter what,
you can run but you cannot hide!
For you will always feel like a piece to the puzzle of your life is missing.
For I am that element missing; one day you will finally see it.
As you grow old in accepted wisdom, you will see how special I was to
you.
Then who knows what road my life would have taken.
I miss you so much, my love.
Through my secret writings, I declared my love to you.
Therefore, I can remember in my journal how special your life has been
to me.
I hope I have given you some special memories as well for you to
remember me by.
A moment in time on which I found the missing part of me.

Is It Really Love?

How do you know if it is really love?
Do you measure it in a meter?
Does a thermometer provide accurate range?
Gauges, gadgets, and measuring tools
Do not provide a maximum value
Do you count the nice things they say?
Do you weight it by how good the sex is?
The caresses, the kisses, and the touch

Do they say they love you many times?
Empty words without restrictions
Just pampering in the heat of the moment
Does pleasure evaluate love?
Because it feels so good
You think it is real
If they have a sexy body then you love
If they like the things you like
You think it's love?
I ask you sarcastically
If they are wild and crazy
Then it is definitely love
If they act like a fool, maybe it's love
If they play mind games, it must be love

The challenge of the pursuit
The hunting of the beast
The challenge of the rebuttal
What happens after the conquest?
What happens after the convincing?
What happens after the attraction dies off?
What happens when it is time to see each other's flaws?
Would you accept my flaws as I accept yours?
Will you get bored of me in an instant?
You do not fit the model I have developed
You do not interest me anymore
I need my space! I am bored!
Games played—is it time to surrender?
What you thought was love

Was it just a game of attraction manipulation?
I want you now; discard you later
Human manhandling for the moment
I thought it was love
What mistakes!
What blindness!
What selfishness!

What is wrong with the word "Love"?
Do not express it if you do not mean it
Do not say it if it is not coming from the heart and mind
Do not reject it when it is real
Do not mistake it for the falsehood of a good time
Illusions, infusions, immorality, inhibitions lowered to the max
To have sex thinking it is love
How good you do me
Determines how much I can love you?
Only in the sacredness of a bedroom
Expressions of unity of two souls
Sharing the intimacy that God intended
To be shared with the one you love
So why misuse it?
Why abused it?
Why treated like it is okay?
To have many different encounters
Confusing love with sex

Love is an expression of the heart and mind
Is the utmost respect for the person that you are
the selfless sacrifice to leave the one you love?
Set it free and let it go
To worry about the one you care for
To pray that he/she is okay
Wish them the best no matter how far
Hope that the love you have for them will never die
Love starts so simple
Like a mustard seed
Tiny speck
Which grows and grows each day
To the tallest trees that reach the skies
Sample of the spiritual growth two souls can ignite

Love can grow without any effort
Love can reach its highest momentum
Even in the isolation of the separation
A test of time
If you think of him/her more than ever
When he/she is far away
That is love!
If the thoughts come more frequently in every moment
Dream of him/her some nights
Even when you tried to get them out of sight
When you cried the tears of sorrow from missing him/her
When you feel like part of you is missing
Heartbroken from not having him/her close by
Missing their companionship
The things they do that will leave others wondering why?
Things which you might find so funny
Acceptance: that is love
Respect: that is love
Partnership: that is love
Companionship: that is love
Acceptance of who they are as a person
Respect their lives and space
Partnership is to discuss things together
Sharing goals and dreams for a future
Companionship is longing for their presence next to you
Even if they are just sleeping next to you
To love is to be free
To accept it
To make a decision to nourish it
To learn how to live with each other
Agreeing to a commitment to share
Learning to enjoy each moment we are together
That is the true expression of Love

It is so easy to make it grow
When you make the decision to accept
In addition, give it back
To be happy for him/her
Encourage, motivate, and cherish
Each other's different interest
Boundaries of respect

It takes teamwork
You and I could make it work
We just have to reach an agreement
Be in the same mentality
Thinking of us as we, me and you, you and I
I am sure that we can survive the test of time
If you learn to love....

I Missed the Chance!

My love, I never got the chance to say how much I really care
Nor even a chance to say face to face I love you and I dare!
I never got the chance to share my dreams, the ones in which you and I
Were to be hand in hand traveling the world to help those in need
How secure I am that You and Me balance each other
I am right next to you to be the comforting shoulder

You did not get a chance to see how pure and loving my heart really is
The love I give to others and the love I have for you
Is a prized gift God made to order
You see, I am not fake because I would not ever know how to pretend
My heart is like a precious gem that shines to give light to others
If only you could see with the eyes of the heart and mind
And see that I love you with my heart, mind, and soul
No doubts, no fears, no regrets
Because it is as real as it gets....

I never got the chance to say how I envisioned you and I growing old
together
How I could see you playing your guitar, bringing joy to children in all
areas
How I see the serious man sharing his story with every man
Who has gone through the very same pain you had to endured
What a great testimony it would be to share how God changed your life

To bring comfort and hope to so many lost souls
I see you sharing skills with many, teaching to do many different things
They otherwise could not afford to do on their own
I see you feeling joy and happiness for being free to do his will
I see you thanking God for giving you a second chance at life
To do what he has planned for you a long time ago; that's why—
I know that what I shared with you has not been an error
Even though your mind still doubts
God put me in your way, for how could you explain
Those beautiful things I said
Without even knowing you when we first communicated?
I know it was God inspired, some words to send you a message of hope

Even to think of the dream that I had when we first began to know each
other
In which I saw you and all you've been through in your life
Tell me, how could you explain that?

I see us on a boat fishing on a beautiful sunny day,
I see us holding each other
Waiting for the sun to set
I see us looking at the stars together
Admiring the immensity of the skies
I see us walking in the sand hand in hand
I see us thinking of how beautiful
It was the day that we met
I see us praying together
Thanking God that we finally found each other

I believe God has a special purpose for the both of us
Imagine how amazing it would be to do God's work together
My faith and hope is in God, who gave me
The realization that spiritual life comes first
And that somehow some individuals
Need to meet each other in the spiritual realm first
Then a decision to love must be made
And a commitment to share your life as well
For if those decisions are not made
The relationship will struggle
For love is an action, not a feeling
You have to make the decision to love
The other person, and then work on it

In my life I have seen that the process of life
Has happened differently to every individual
To some it happens fast and swift
To some slow and lengthy
The manner in which it happens also is different; it could be
Orderly and practically predictable
And to others scattered and mixed up
To teach a lesson on self-discovery
Because some individuals need to shape certain
Things in their character in order to learn
How to appreciate the other partner

This transformation is more essential than any physical attraction
For real love is growing together spiritually
And helping each other see and reach the momentum of insight
In reverence for God and in reverence for life
Last of all, in reverence for each other

The Soul Connection ...

Your face has left a reflection on my heart so clear
And vivid like it was just yesterday
Your soul had connected with mine close but yet so far
Your spirit touched me swiftly, so smooth and pure caresses
Your heart I saw the very first moment we talked
And to this day I still don't know why
Your mind I have known, because I challenged it and admired the man
you are
I love who you are as a person and respect what you choose to be
I know it might sound crazy but you are whom I seek
I feel like I've known you at another life and dimension
I feel like I was yours, and at times I can sense your presence here with
me
I sense I have known you in the past
And cannot quite pinpoint where
Your face is so familiar that I sense the smell of your skin
Your scent I have known before and your touch I have felt as well
Our bodies had intertwined in passionate lovemaking
Two lost souls
Reaching heavenly ecstasy with an insatiable hunger
That by just looking at each other we can ignite the passion
That can light the fire and send off the sparks of a once true love
I believed we were one during those precious moments
Two lost souls who had made a connection

Ever Been In Love?
Part III A Prayer for Us

Dear Soul Mate:

I write so that one day I will have the wonderful memories that I once came in touch with the man of my dreams; but love did not stop for me.

I pray each day to forget you and all the memories of your serious face, which is inscribed in my heart and soul.

No particular reason can I give to explain, no special clues to give for myself; I am left dazed and confused.

I swear I never meant to fall in love with you; unbeknownst to me I did with no explanations of when and how.

No, it's not an infatuation, I know how that feels; no, it's not a crush—I am not a young girl anymore.

It's the mature love that comes with experience which allows you to accept all the flaws, imperfections, and many other things as well.

To love unconditionally without expecting anything back. The strong sense of security of not having to worry if you are with someone else, because in my heart I know you are true to me.

With the utmost admiration for the person that you are, I respect all that you are with no doubts in my mind.

To accept the life you live and give you all your space, my hope, wishes, and dreams are locked inside my heart, although my soul yearns to be with my other half.

I do not strive, for who am I to know if one day our paths will cross again? Starting fresh like new, maturity will be our mediator and experience our common ground.

We both were not able to find the very same thing we have been looking for all along, but all at the wrong times.

For love is patient and I will wait for the man who has stirred up all my emotions that I had been holding in

You opened up some senses that were long lost, and now I am left lost in love.

You can ask, "Who is this soul mate?" He is my partner and other half! It is he who feels what I am feeling, and thinks that same way too. He is also my companion for life.

We both had similar experiences in life; therefore, we are meant to be—we can complement each other with no effort. Help each other grow spiritually as well.

For anyone can take the place of a boyfriend, lover, and even wife or husband but lack the most important thing: the skill to be a partner and a friend.

My soul mate, he is all....

Sincerely,

Your partner & friend

I Am Blessed

I am blessed, for I have known love
It came to me so unexpectedly
Without a warning or premeditation
A deep feeling grew in my heart and soul
I have never experienced such an emotion
My mind is his to be known
Deep in sentiment, mystified, and yearning to be his
I left him alone for him to make his own decision
Be wild and free

No attachment
No remembrance
No way I can make him see
What is in my heart and mind?

The love I feel
How much I care
Are questions that only I can answer
For he is not in contact with me anymore
His mind and heart are somewhere else

Only fond memories of those special moments we spent together
I cannot get them out of my mind
I relive the memories without any effort
Feels like just yesterday we were together
How free I felt
How comfortable feeling
So natural
Like I have been his before

I felt so secure in his arms
I felt so wanted
I felt so loved
Our intimacy has been an experience stored in my heart
For the man of my dreams
Has been close to me
His hands and his caresses provided me so much warmth
Being close to his heart
Becoming one

How much I miss this closeness
How much I miss his kisses
How much I miss his scent
How much I miss caressing his dark hair
How much I miss watching him fall asleep

I cannot explain what I feel
I tried to forget him to no avail
I am stuck in his sweet caresses
For he is the missing part of me
That other piece that is missing
No matter if he believes or not
He means so much more to me

I did not plan it this way
I did not want to have to experience distress
I did not want to have to miss someone so much it hurts
I dream of him at night
He is an admirable man in my eyes

I know that he can be so much more to me
For I have seen what he can be
My darling, I wish you could see the beauty of my love for you
That I am willing to let you go, be wild, and free
With room to grow
Only the Lord knows what is in the future

I really wish that you could see
Seek me out and you will see
You will not regret what you have found
For you will find true, enduring love
Will last a lifetime if you let it be
Grow old together hand in hand
Watching you play your old guitar
Remembering the day that we first met

I promise you, love of my life
That I will be true only to you
I am the woman of your dreams

The one that will love you forever
Keep you safe and warm within my arms
Show you the love you never had
I will be your companion to listen to
Be your loving partner when you need a hug or two
I will be your lover, never get tired of our intimacy
For every day will be a new experience for you and me

I want to reach new heights, new goals
And share all my dreams with you
I am so secure with how I feel
That I am here and by myself
Do not worry at all; my faith lies in God
Because I learned that you cannot hurry love
However, I feel lonely because I miss you so
I need a shoulder to lean on
Do not wait too long to realize that it has been me all along
Whom you should have been close to
Remember that life goes on and I might just decide not to wait any
longer
One day I will vanish out of your sight

I Wish

I wish that I could have shared with you
Before going our separate ways what has happened in my life
I did not have the courage to tell you
That I had found God when I reached this location
I've been saved, my life has changed
And this is the reason why
There is a separation between us
You see, God knows that I have made a pact
To keep my self pure for my soul mate
And I have to be an example to you
Show you that I will no longer abuse my temple

I decided finally to do things right in my life
Especially now since nothing else has worked for me
I have decided instead to wait
And live my life in purity
Why now?
Why at my age?
Why did I make this decision?

Now I realize that if I want a man to respect me
I need to respect myself first
I am forty years old; I deserve to find my soul mate
Why? Because as long as I keep being self-indulgent
I will not be taken seriously
Why share your intimacy with someone
Who does not have any plans to share life with you
Or commitment to respect you
It's like a prize given to someone even though they don't deserve it
I now understand how valuable it really is
And I feel great about it
Don't regret the decision of my celibacy
Look forward to that someone who will appreciate me for being me
No looking back, no giving up—look forward to
Meeting my soul mate in purity

<u>Hoping</u> ...

I keep hoping that one day he will come back ...
I want to see him again face to face
I yearn for his caresses and sweet kisses on my face
I miss him altogether and hope that he is well
I wonder what has happened and hope to know the truth

No signs of him or his acknowledgement of me ever, yet again
Silence is fear controlling the freedom to love
Prisoner of yourself you've become
Letting your pride get in your way instead
Too proud to tell me, hey there was something great between us
Something so amazing and unexpected

That day when we met was so real, like yesterday
In hope of finding a friend, I found my soul mate instead
I looked into your eyes and there stood the man of my dreams
The one I always dreamed about and knew one day would be here for me
The reflection of your face I had already known
Your smell, your touch, and even the sound of your voice
Familiar as the morning sun

How was I able to know that you were the one?
How am I so sure that it is you I am living for?
How come every day and night that passes by I miss you more and more?
Not seeing you is killing me so deep inside my soul
My mind is tortured by the memories of the days we were so close
As if it was just yesterday you held me in your arms
As if it was just today you kissed my lips passionately

To know that the only man my body yearns for is you
And that no one else can do for me
What you have made me discover
If only you can believe that my soul,
Heart and mind belong to you
And only you
Baby, no one else can accomplish this
You have stolen my heart
Swept away my mind and thoughts

My soul yearns, for you to return
And meet me where I am
Check it out for yourself
See that it is true
That my heart and mind belong to you
No one else can take your place

Believe me when I say this
You are the one I hope to settle down with
The one I can see myself growing old together with
The one that I can care for as years go by
And say honey, I love you so much today just like yesterday
You brought to me hope and faith in the future
Have shared with you some unforgettable memories
I relive those moments as if it just happened today
I appreciated so much your care and affection
Love you for you
Not for what you can give me
Accepted you as you are
No need to change anything
For I love you for who you are

The ocean has become my amulet of faith
As the waves come and go
One day you too will come my way
The sun has become my horizon of hope
That will clear your path
Lead you to my door
Find your way back home my love
For I am waiting for you with open arms
Free your mind—free your spirit
To accept for once in your lifetime
You found your best friend and soul mate

You will never regret it, I promise you this much
With no shame or regrets, I declare this to you
I am what your heart has been waiting for
I am what your mind has been hoping to meet
I am what your soul needs and I complete you
And you complete me

Claribel Coreano

I wish that you could finally see
Open the eyes of your soul instead
Open your mind to accept
Open your heart to receive my love
Free yourself from fear and pride
Humbly accept my love as a gift from the soul
Teach you that in life, love does exist
And you can find it in the simplest things

If you are free enough to declare to someone
How much you love and care for them
It is because you know yourself well enough
Love yourself enough
To love someone with your heart and mind
This spontaneous act is as real as it gets
Don't shy away from love
For superficial sex
Empty gratification that many can give to you
But real love does not happen every day
Once in a lifetime you are lucky enough to find it
But it can easily be lost with pride
If you let your unrealistic ways get in the way
Don't demand so much
Don't look for what is not real
People pleasers can be what you want them to be
Forfeiting themselves to make someone else happy
I, however, let go and let the truth be revealed
I am free to be me and this is accepted by me

For your pride is stronger than you
Remember that as time goes by and you deny my love
Someday soon enough you will miss my love
That day it will become all clear to you
That day maybe too late for me I'm afraid
I will ignore you like you have done to me
You will discover that what comes around goes around
Play the scene in your life like the one I had the chance to take part in
Heartbroken, you will remember me and say I wish that I would have
sought her then
Now I have lost her and it will never be the same
I hope that there is time left for you and me someday!

216

Long-Distance Love

I miss you even though I never met you face to face
I threw your pictures away long ago
And still I can remember exactly how you look
Your face is on my mind, haunting me day after day
I wish I could forget you and not remember you
But my mind plays tricks and my heart deceives me as well
For they constantly remind me it's him whom you love
Don't fight it even though he doesn't know
How hard is it to know that you love a man whom you have never seen?
How the hell did I let this happen? And what a foolish woman you are
For falling in love with a stranger who never seeks your love
Missing you like heck just wanting to hear your voice; I am a wreck
And miss you dearly every day, hoping always you are okay and miss me
as well
Please, God, erase this man from my heart; I can't bear it any longer
Let him be just a sweet, nostalgic memory, for this will help me overcome
This love I have for this man who never will send his love back my way

Dear Friend

It's hard to accept that you are no longer in my life, a friend I believe
had.
I miss the sound of your voice, I miss the laughter, and I miss your
silliness.
I do not know what has happened between us; you have separated
yourself from me.
I can't understand why you could not even say good-bye
Or give a reason of why you have vanished out of my life.

I can't let go, for you are still in my heart,
You are in my mind day in day out.
My heart feels the pain of your isolation.
I dream of you almost every night
I miss you so much, dear friend, I wish you could understand.
I am not sure what has happened to me but I fell in love with you.
No warning I felt,
Did not know that it could happen to me.

I was not ready for it,
But the feeling has not left me; I love you and it is genuine.
For I have never experienced myself in these circumstances,
Never knew love this deep existed.
It is a God-given love for one person unconditionally
Accepting another individual without any prejudice or restrictions.

All I know is that you are in my heart and mind.
I pray for you each night
That God can guide you and touch your soul.
To know that there is a special someone who waits for your return,
My dear friend, I wish you could see past all the obstacles in your way,
See with the spiritual eyes in their place.

See my heart.
Connect with my mind.
Accept me just as I am.
Share with me your life in a good way.

Be willing to share a pledge of partnership,
That we can respect each other and love only each other,
Become the best of friends, partner, and lovers.

For you and I are no mistake.
Tell your mind not to debate.
Give in, my friend, you won't regret.

Take time to know me well.
I am what your heart has been yearning for.
I am what your soul has been waiting for.
I am what your mind has been contemplating.
I am the friend you've always sought after.
I am that passionate lover you always dream of.
I am the sweetness of your days,
That we may both grow old together
And reminisce that we started off as friends
And became one together.
Dear friend, I miss you, please come back to me again.

A Prayer for My Friend

Lord, you know everything; nothing hidden is reserved, secret
throughout life
By your word, tell us that whatever is done in the darkness
Will become known one day and come to light
Face your inner conflicts, face the past, and change your character
Not until you accept the issues at hand
Will you feel that you have to hide in secret
Guilt, shame, and resentment keep you from moving on
Hatred deep rooted inside your heart keeps you enslaved to your rage
The heaviness of your heart that is weighing you down
To feel that pleasure is the only way
To erase your pain and make you feel like a man

Your father, who hurt you so bad
You hate him for his behavior
Resent him for leaving you
Angry because he hurt you
Scarred you for life with pain
Never once did he say I am sorry, Son!
I did not mean to cause you pain and grief
Too bad I was not a good example for you to follow
Sorry that your image of a father is tainted
I hurt you bad, my son; please forgive me
Let us make amends and continue in our life in forgiveness

Dear friend, it seems that you go on in life stuck in the stage of a
teenager
You do not want to grow up you refuse to mature;
You can not get away from your rebellious nature
You were taught at an earlier age to hate and hold on to grudges
Your father was not there for you during your most important days
Neglected and abused you; never acknowledge your pain

My friend, accept what your father did. I am pretty sure that in his old
age
He has been miserable; his heart is giving up because it is full of regrets
of the pain he caused others whom he thought were in his way
I believe that he has finally accepted Jesus in his heart

And knows now the pain he caused
He has to deal with it day in and day out.
Courage he does not have, because he is too ashamed to ask you
forgiveness
Although he knows deep down in his heart that God has forgiven him
In addition, wants him to make amends with you someday
However, why wait until he is on his deathbed?
Why not deliver yourself from this enslavement?

Be courageous and ask for his forgiveness
Even though you were not the one at fault
You will see how this can help you heal and let go of all the pain
Friend, your father is not the cause of your pleasure-seeking behavior
Nor is he the one that tells you every day, "Son, you are weak
Therefore, you do not meet the world's expectations"
Use this; it will make you feel numb
Make you forget, at least for time being
The pain you carry in the baggage of your heart and mind

With all my heart and soul, my friend
I wish that you could investigate your deep-rooted sin
Which is keeping you constrained by this hurting
That you are constantly trying daily to sedate in order to forget what you
need to face

How can you say that your are "free"
When you feel that you have to look for your father's love in someone
else?
You have mistaken your identity
Question your daily existence
You do not know who you really are deep inside of your heart
You are scared of commitment
Terrified of intimacy
Afraid to be the man that you are destined to be
Moreover, the man God wants you to become
Because of past mistakes

Tell me why I have visions of all that you have gone through in your life
Please explain why I see what you are constantly fighting in your present
I am scared for you; I am in deep sorrow for you
I love you so much because I have seen what you have gone through in
your life
Dear friend, how do I even begin to tell you that our connection is of the
spiritual kind?
I have seen your heart and mind without even having to question you
I do not know why but I am worried about your future
You see, the Lord is trying to tell you that it is time for you to break free

Nevertheless, your anger, resentment, and egotistical behavior keep you
trapped in sin
You know it better than me, but you do not want to stop sinning
You do not want to listen to God! You do not want to listen to what he is
asking of you
How can you say no to God? My heart aches just thinking of how lonely
your life will be
Not to have God's grace upon you because of pride
Remember, time is passing; a stopwatch in heaven doesn't exist
Our destiny we cannot control; only God knows how many days we have
I am not sure why I have to be frank, but time is running out for you
If you lose his presence due to worldly gains and pleasure
You have forfeited your soul to the devil and the battle has been won on
his part
I wish I could make you understand how amazing God has been in my
life
I have found the joy I needed, and realized that it is not material, fame,
fortune, pleasure
Or money that can fulfill someone's heart
It is the love of God that can finally set us free
I am praying, my dear friend, that time will not be too late for you
That you can realize the sins of your heart and accept the Lord in your
heart
Make amends with yourself and with others as well
My prayers from the heart and soul
To my dear friend who does not know God's love
Please listen to God's calling before it becomes too late to answer Him

Apology

My love, I apologize
Did not mean to offend you in any way
I just wanted make you understand
That even though we are far apart you are still inside my heart and mind
I can't stop thinking of the wonderful times we shared
It was so amazing in my life to share those moments with you
The more I tried to get them out of my mind
The more the constant memories come up
I know that we were not a mistake
Something so amazing happened to me that day
I became part of you somehow
It's like part of me is missing because you are not here with me

How can I explain what I feel?
Don't know where to begin
I know that I cannot entice you to come to me
Nor will I use my womanly senses to bring you close to me
Sex is only powerful temporarily
I am a woman of class, too secure to think it is the only way to your heart
I am past all of the worldly ways; sinful nature is a mistake

I have not given up on you
I just want you to be sure
Experience in your heart and mind before you draw closer to me
I know that other women will pass your way, and many tricks they will
play
They will possibly make you think
And believe that they are the one; you will see!
But a façade they will provide and a distraction to your heart
You will try to convince your heart and mind to forget me
But to no avail, because my love is stronger than theirs

The only way I can assure myself that
God can guide you is through prayer
I pray for you each day that you can be saved
I love you so much that all I can hope for you
Is that you can have a personal relationship with God
Finally see the things He wants for you

Be set free from all your bondage
A new life in Christ you will begin
A loving heart God will place
Your mind will be healed as well
Then you will remember the woman
Who was spiritually chosen to grow with you
I believe in miracles and this one I will not ignore
I know my heart is pure and my faith is greater than the both us
My Lord hears my prayers
He will bring my soul mate back to me with an open mind
And with an open heart
Willingly be open to respect me and committed to spending the rest of
his life with me

It's So Nice To Hear Your Voice

It was soothing to hear your voice; just a hello can do it
I miss you so much; it was clearly identifiable
But just the hello can break me free
From the sadness that I was feeling
You didn't know that you called at the right time
For just last night I prayed that you would
Change your mind and call me anyway
For I have been experiencing some tribulations
And hoping you would feel my pain
Seek me anyway

In all humbleness I cannot keep a grudge
For I love to share with people
And you are so special to me
That I will take the time to set
Matters aside as long as you can see
That what happened between you and me
Was just a childish issue

I wish you and I could understand each other
As I understand you and often feel you're hurting
Reach and connect with me spiritually
You will find the connection there
You just have to reach out to me
I never in my life thought this could happen to me
Feel so close to someone even though you are far away

The strange things that happen to me late at night
I awake at 2:50, 3:00, and sometimes at 4:00 a.m.
And I feel that you are awake as well
I get the urge to call you right at those very same times
It's like our souls need some connection right then at those points
It's weird to feel this way, and how could I even began to explain?
But the first thing that comes to my mind when I wake
Is "He is awake, call him up; his spirit needs you to connect"
But then I fear that you might think I am wacky
For calling you so early in the morning

And I back up, but it gets really hard to go back to sleep
Because maybe it was your voice that I needed to hear
To give some warmth and to feel you close, then sleep will be near

I Miss You ...

*I miss you; it's hard to get used to the idea that you are no longer in my
life,*
The friend whom I thought would learn to love me and stick it out.
What drove you away? The fear that you might fall in love?
The fear that I may be the one? But you are just too stubborn to know!
You let your pride and the mumbo jumbo philosophy you believe
Dictate what is real and what is not. Don't question life so much!
Why can't you understand that real love exists? It's not a perfected
*solution to one of your mathematical equations, and let me tell you that it
does balance out.*
*Don't keep going in circles trying to solve it, or hitting your head against
the wall*
Trying to be perfect! It will not happen the way you want!
It's not like the fantasy you have in your mind.
The checklist doesn't exist here
Nor the 34, 23, 36 measurements.
You can't clone it if you wish!
It's not for you to judge; it's for you to seek.
It's the action that you take to accept someone as they are,
To become open-minded and say, "Hey, this can work."
Let me tell you, it is not the beauty, nor the intelligence, nor the money,
Nor the great family the individual comes from.
It's the decision to love in spite of it all,
To care for someone and be interested in who they are.
It is to accept me as I accept you as well,
To know that we are not perfect and we all make mistakes.
Tell me, what gives you the right to ignore a love such as mine?
Why can't you be brave and say, "Can we talk and get to know me closer,
And find out who I really am"?
You live in your own space and time,
Closed world only to whom you care to keep out.
Why can't you open the doors and let me in?
What can I take from you that you are so troubled?
I am not here to take anything from you
But to share my heart with you.
I do not want what you cannot give.
I want to learn what growth we can reach.
I don't want to be pampered.

Claribel Coreano

I want to be understood.
I don't want anything material.
I just want your love instead.
I am not asking for much.
I miss you dearly, my love.

Memories

i

I arrived in the state of Missouri early in the afternoon
Rented a car from the airport to my destination
After driving for three hours on the famous, historic Route 66
Mountains, hills, a long road with beautiful sceneries
Saw horses, cows, and many wineries
I appreciated the beautiful skies and sceneries as I passed by
In the small city of St. Roberts I arrived
I rented a room at the local Econo Lodge

Trying to save money
For I did not have much to spare
I opened the door to the room, and as I looked around
I realized that the room looked exactly like the one we once had shared
From the curtains to the bedspread, it was all the same thing
As if by déjà vu I relived the same scenes
Thinking back to the times when you and I were close

As the memories floated by
I felt a great feeling of loneliness
Overwhelmed with sadness
I looked around to see two well-made beds without any signs of anyone
sleeping in them
I realized that I was all alone
In an empty room without my best friend there with me
I was starting to feel sad
Remembering the times you and I had shared
Some fun moments together
As tears began flowing I became aware of how much I miss you

How much I wish you could have been there with me
Lying next to me with my head closely nestled in your arms
I felt so brokenhearted
I could not contend with my emotions
How could this be?
The man whom I shared so many specials moments with
Has vanished without a good-bye
No signs of him any longer

His scent I could still sense around me
The warmness of just laying next to him, caressing his dark hair
His smile, his silliness and wittiness
I missed him all around me
Missing him in everything I saw in that cold and desolate room
For how could he just turn away from me like that
As if nothing had ever happened between us?
Why is it so easy for him not to miss me?
I think to myself, why did I not mean anything to him?
Nevertheless, he has meant so much to me
Why do I have no closure, no good-byes?
I feel as though we have unfinished business
At least a respectful conversation between two adults
To tell me the truth of the what and why you have distanced yourself
from me

ii

For I deserve the truth; I am not an ignorant woman
I demand the truth, for no matter what you think or what your mind
perceives
I am real, I have nothing to hide, and if you needed to know something
about me
All you needed was to ask

I am hurting; I am in pain, for missing him is killing me
I heard that people can die of being heartbroken
I now understand why!
I feel as though I had been married to him long ago
And he left me in grief
Now I have a dying soul
I know that I am different
I am not like other women
I am not a sex machine
Nor a pleasure-seeking individual
Yes, it is true I am somewhat naïve
But I have accepted me and am happy to be me
All I need is for you to learn how to understand me

I am not one to go out of my way to seek a man
I can't; I am too classy for that
Do not get me wrong; I am humble not conceited

I do not think that is the way to do things
I do, however, deserve your attention and connection
Respect in the same way as I view you
Humanness demands that you treat others as you want to be treated
Even the simplest individual who in your view is insignificant
Measure your perfectionist standards
Like a scale, like a thermometer, or high blood pressure gauge
You always see them as a zero
For in your world they have to measure high

For what you see is only on the outside
Don't be mistaken or overlook, for what you seeking is not the truth
Superficiality is what you see
Living a daydream in a fantasy land
Hoping for fame, you stand with no regret
No remorse for whom you leave behind
As long as you continue to seek your own ambition
Stand aside, no time to stop and no time left to love back
You are rushing into self-destruction emotionally

You seek and seek like a humming bird for new flowers
Eat the nectar from all the beautiful flowers
Discard them as I go along, no time to look back and even say hello
You will one day grow old and see
That the most beautiful flower you have ignored
Was the sweetness of your dreams
The one who could have been there in your golden age
Still caressing your graying hair
Loving you in spite of the wrinkles, slumps, and weakness
So humble a love that the only wish I have is to grow old with you

How Come?

How come I have not been able to forget you?
How come you are still in my dreams?
How come I still can see you in my thoughts?
How come my sleep is disturbed because I still feel your warmth at night?
How come when I think about you I still cry?
How come I miss you more and more each passing day?
How come I yearn to be with you instead of forgetting you?
How come each day instead of losing hope I gain faith?
How come I still feel that you and I were not a mistake?
How come I can almost see the future that awaits us?
How come I can see past the wall that separates us?

To break free I have tried everything
I am a prisoner of your spirit and warmth
My mind has been trying to delete thoughts and memories
My heart fights with all its might to get you out of the deepest roots of emotion
That have captured my heart with a force that not even I can fight
To feel when you are sad and lonesome
To know that I know each moment when you're hurting
Feeling what you're feeling
As if you are talking to me via telepathy
I know that I am that shining light that can light that dark path you are walking into
I know what can set you free from the turmoil that you are feeling
I am just a guiding soul to lead you to the peace your heart needs
Your guardian angel and soul mate
Who knows exactly what you are missing

You know the truth and still you don't seek it
You know the answer and still you debate it
You know the road and still you are lost
You know the peace you need to follow is the peace that comes from God
You know that the humbleness in me and unconditional love
Haunts you day in and day out
It's hard to see the light

It's hard to see the way
It's hard to accept that it is me you need
It's hard to accept the truth of what I told you

The knowledge of knowing that someone has told you the truth about you
Honest enough not to lie about it
Trying to make you see the purpose for living
Trying to make you understand that God is the ultimate answer
Trying to make you see that it's worth the risk
You will see that it's you and me that were meant to be
I know now more than ever that it is you who I need in my life
I know now more than ever that I will not give up the fight
I know now more than ever that I will not lose my hope in us
I look forward more and more each day to being with you
I know now that you will have to hit rock bottom
Turn around and think about your mistakes
See with the clarity of our souls
The blindness will be lifted
Your mind will be set free
Your heart will be cured from pain
Think freely
Your soul will lead you to mine

You will find the peace of heart through God
I will always pray for you, my love
That soon we can share special times
I miss you dearly and I can't wait to see you
Hold me in your arms and see you smile
Your heart beating next to mine
I think it is all worth the wait….

Good-Bye

Never got the chance to say my final good-bye
I attempted to, but when I looked in your eyes
I just couldn't depart
I tried many times but I can't detach
Although I need the closure in my life
How many times must I cry tears of sorrow?
To finally forget you?
But when I think I have just accomplished it
I remember the day at sea
When we were together, so happy still
Memories come to mind like pictures
Just being taken
Remember the big fish we caught
Remember the picture I took
Remember the smile on your face
I knew that it was not a fake
There was joy and pure happiness
We were a great team together
The clearness of the water I still see in my mind
Hues of blues, corals, and aqua as the boat made its way to the deep
ocean
The clarity of the skies, the puffiness of the clouds
The sun radiant and shiny, guiding us to the horizon
How beautiful a memory I still hold in my mind clear as day, but your
shadow still fades away
How beautiful the moments
We shared that day
Fate took us into an exploration of Mother Nature
I felt like a child in love with the sea
Marveled at everything that I did see
How can you say that it was just a fling?
When that week we spent together
Was as magical as the sea?
For every time we talked we always were mesmerized about our vacation
Two of us together, memories in synchronization
You read my mind and I read yours
Answered your questions before you got the chance to ask
If it was a mistake

How come it felt so great?
If it was an error
How come I don't regret it?
If it was just a phase
How come I can still remember every single detail?

Things just don't happen to happen
There is meaning to us
There is a story to tell
Wonderful memories that I preserve
There are other pages in our book that need to be filled
And even though you are not here with me
Or think that you don't care
I still do not believe that this is the way you feel
See, what happened between us was real as the day and night
Two souls on a quest for each other that day
There is a greater meaning
There is a better ending
There is still hope in my heart
That my partner and fishing buddy
Will humbly accept someday soon
That we are not a mistake

It's a miracle of God that I love you the way I do
Unconditional acceptance, understanding, and patience
Don't reject what you have been searching all your life
Because of pride
Don't neglect the love that is in my heart for you
And ask why? Don't let yourself be guided by your stubbornness
Thinking that our friendship
Could not turn into the most amazing love
Ever experienced

Give up already
You're fighting too hard
Struggling to forget me
Searching in others for everything I got
What happens when they cannot give you anything back?
You will find yourself alone
Thinking back on our sweet memories

Claribel Coreano

Wishing hard to find what we once had
The best thing in your life
You have let it slip away
Too proud to accept
Too selfish to give back

But my heart humbly accepts
That you are not coming back
That all I have are these wonderful memories
That still lingers on in my mind
I wait barefoot in the ocean
For my captain to arrive
Waving with my hands
Trying to give you a sign
To stop and come back to me

Ever Been In Love?
Part IV Closure

<u>In Life</u>

In life you take your chances
A chance too, like many
But in true love?
You only get to love once
By chance if you could find the one
Whose heart you think you own
By chance if they can provide the same amount of love
By chance if you can keep them
By chance if they want to stay
In life you take your chances
Hoping that every chance you take
Can bring you closer and closer to the one that will not go away
A chance to love with all your heart and soul
That only happens once by chance if it is with the right one
So by chance I will go on my life's journey
By chance I will endure my loss
Because by chance I fell in love
With my one and only true love

Too bad that by chance I wasn't his to be known
So sad that my only chance at love was with my once-in-a-lifetime true
love

Who never knew that by chance I truly and forever would love him?
By chance he lost out to see that if he took the chance I might have been
His once in a lifetime as well ...
And so the story goes....
In life you take your chances and I took mine at love
My chance was used previously
And there will never be another chance
To love as deeply and truly
Like the risk I took with you
My once in a lifetime, just one chance in life
I had to love you as deep and true
Like the love I have in my heart for you
Once in a lifetime ... it happened to me

People Tell Me ...

People tell me that I am a fool for loving you
They think I am crazy for saving myself for you
I have heard many times that you don't deserve my love
You are not worth me waiting for your return
That you are selfish and self-centered
Don't know how to appreciate a classy woman like me

But who are they to judge what is inside my heart and mind?
For this love even I was not able to stop
I have often thought of the many reasons that you don't deserve my
attention
As hard as it is, my mind and heart tell me don't give up on him
I wait in silence like a fool for you to return to me
Every moment, no matter how much I try not to think of you
Still thoughts creep in my mind....

I tried many times to forget you ...
I try to control my mind and heart
My spirit yearns for your return
Hoping to see you again
There is no peace within my soul
I yearn to be held by you
I yearn to be kissed by you
I yearn to be touched by you
Feel your warmth
See your smile
Caress your hair
Fall asleep in my arms
Wake up next to me
Talk until the sun comes up again
Make love until daybreak

Yes, I am a fool for loving you
But one thing I know is that I will never give up on you
You are my soul mate, this I know
No other man can take your place
For my heart and mind belong only to you
Many can ask if you deserve this pure and unconditional love

239

*My only answer is that he has won the prize of a loving partner and
friend
Who understands him like a book
Know him so well in such a short time
A difficult man he says he is
But in my eyes it is just stubbornness I see
Trying to be strong and heartless
But deep inside sweet memories live
Thoughts of me still linger on....
The smell of my scent he still breathes
The warmth of my soul*

*He still feels.... Although he denies it, even swears it is not true
My sweetness and my loving ways
he can not forget, in fact he yearns for them still
He misses me like I miss him
Too proud to see the truth
And still goes around
Debating in his heart and mind
That no ... this can't be
What a struggle not to give in
So scared and fearful to love so deep
My darling, I know the feeling too....
Before I met you I was feeling the same thing*

*But I have set myself free and experienced the best thing in my life
To love so pure and simple
That nothing matters as long as you are all right
The feeling, the thoughts, my heart, my mind, my soul, and spirit
All belong to you....
So much respect I have in my heart for you*

*I am still waiting for you to make up your mind
And come back to me with open arms
I wait for your return
Like a fool blinded by love
Desire only you, to be by your side
Share things I never felt with like sharing with anybody else
You bring out the best in me
You make my dark days into sunny days
Sharing my life with you is what I hope for*

Hold your hands until I grow old
See those brown eyes until my last blink
Watch you grow old next to me
Take care of you when you feel sick
Provide you with warmth and love to last for the rest of your life

My hope is waiting to share with you
My dreams, my hopes, my goals, my wants, my desires
And accomplish it with you by my side
I am not so hard to please—all I want is your companionship
We can be the best of friends
The best of lovers all over again
This affection isn't over, it's just begun to play
My darling, please give up your selfish pride
Come back to me
I wait with open arms
To hold you again close to my heart....
I don't care what people think

It's not a crime to accept my heart and mind
It's not a sin to love so deep like what's in my heart for you
A fool who loves you indiscreetly, in silence, in secret
Without any shame or fear or regret
Just waiting for the day that you accept my heart and mind
And love me just the same
A fool's prophecy in love we will be
Just in time for us this moment in time....

I Gave You the Best of Me

I gave you the best of me and you took and took
Till you could have no more
To you it was a game
To me it was a special time
My friend, I learned to love you
And that was my downfall
For I became your friend
And saw so deeply inside your heart
Felt so secure, and a future near
But to you it was nothing
Although it is never clear

Another relationship without substance
That is what you say and want to see
For you are not easily satisfied
Because what you want is so unreal
Perfection doesn't exist
Not unless you want a robot
But I am just a simple woman
Without anything to make amends for

For I believe in you
Gave you all my trust
Now I am lost in love
The pain I can no longer endure
For you took for granted
The best thing that has happened to you
For in fact in your life you have found
The "real thing" but you let it go
Because it was not perfection at its best

In fact you want much more
I cannot give you what you are looking for
Because what you are looking for it so unreal
The image that you present is something that you are not
I am down to earth; no need to pretend—for what?
I don't believe in pleasing people
Or living life under someone else's dreams

For their success is theirs, not mine
Nor will they acknowledge you or me
Remember, you've been used and abused
Stop giving to others who will never value you
Learn to give to those who will respect you
There are simple people out there who will show
More care and appreciation
Stop wasting so much time
Learn to stop pleasing people
You are #1
And only you can make a difference

It Is So Easy to Give Up

I could have given up on you, a long time ago
But I just couldn't
I thought about it
But then I would have been like everyone else in your life
But I am not going to
I am different

I love you and this is the truth
I can't give up on you
For love is patient and love is kind
True love endures forever
Real love doesn't give up hope
That one day a miracle may happen

I love you unconditionally without any reservations
You cannot measure the love I have for you
I know that it sounds old-fashioned
To be in love with someone who is so far away
I know it is true because my heart is faithful only to you
I save myself in pureness because you are the only man
That I will ever become intimate with
So sacred a pact I have made with myself
That no other man can fit in your shoes or even replace you

You are the man of my dreams
You are the one my heart beats for
You are the one I want to spend the rest of my life with
I know you, I understand you, I respect you, and I cherish you
I want the best for you; I would love to share my life with you
I want you to grow spiritually and become what you were meant to be
I pray for you, I worry about you, and I know that you are part of me
Even though you are far away

Half of me is missing; part of me is gone away
You are the other half that completes me in a way
So special are you to me that
I cannot bear the pain of missing you each day
I cry each night because I miss you so much

I wish you could be with me instead
But only if your mind and heart is ready
Only if you want to respect me
Only if you want to share your life with me the same
I love you and that is not a mistake
It is a miracle of life that we both needed in a sense

This Is For You!

To anyone who has loved with your heart and soul
I dedicate this to you
A sweet memoir of memories
Of the love you lost
Remembrance of the first kiss
You felt on your lips
From the one who stole your heart and mind
I can relate to your pain and can almost feel your sorrow
For I have also loved in the very same way

Sometimes we do not stay with the one we love
Sometimes they go away like a feather flying by
The wind reminds us of their presence
Their warmth and of their scent
A brush with stolen love
Moments gone
No telling how

It was special when we had them near
Appreciated every moment with them
Embracing our souls
Love till there is no tomorrow
Gone within the next day
Forgotten with our sorrows
That never go away

Each day I think of him
Like you may think of her or him
Thoughts and memories to live by
Wishing that they can come back
But gone away, far away
They left with no regrets
Or good-byes
Just a shadow passing by

No one likes to stay for very long
These days relationships are temporarily
As long as you get your groove on

Morals, values, or romanticism
Of yesteryears exist no more
It's just a bore

Could not give back the love we gave them
Nor even stay to see if it can grow
Instead
Escape, too difficult to accept that I love him
Too compromising knowing someone cared
Too scared of a thought to settle down
Too proud to think of me somehow
That someone can love you
Without expecting anything in return
Just your respect, communication
Sharing the special moments
Dedicating time to making it work
Then love will grow like a rose
If you invest in something so beautiful
Then you will be sure to get something back
For love grows and grows when two souls share of each other
Teaching one another to accept who they are
Compromise
Respect
Communicate
And
Eternal partnership
That will last a lifetime
That is what our love could have been
It is not a grocery shopping list
You need them to look a certain way
You need to have this instead
You need to be young and free
Wild and open to do as you please
No boundaries to set
Just a good time to experiment
No need to think that love is an investment
Only a secret rendezvous
Sharing stolen moments
Then forgetting
That once you become intimate

It is a sacred union
Not a tension releaser
But an expression of love
Made by God for two souls
To unite and become one
Union of souls that knows love
Can last a lifetime
At least that was what I thought!

How Do I Let You Go?

Tell me, how do I let you go if you are constantly on my mind?
The memories keep haunting me day and night—I see you in every
beautiful thing that I see, because in my heart you are that to me.

I try and I try with no success; tell me, how do I let you go? When at
night I still feel your touch and your scent has not yet left my pillow, the
pain is so intense that I often cry myself to sleep. My sorrow is so deep
that it is reminiscent of death.

Why did it have to end this way? Why couldn't things stay the same?
But I know I must let you go—because your heart was never mine, and,
unlike you, my heart will still be yours until the end of time.

I will let you go! I will let you be free, I will set you free like a dove in
the middle of spring, who spreads his wings on the horizon to soar to
new heights in liberty. I will set you free like the first snow flake that falls
in the winter, the one that is usually the biggest, its flurries the brightest
but disappearing so quickly.

I will set you free like a shooting star that shoots across the universe, that
lights up the darkness of immense space. Lucky are those who can get to
see such a spectacular sight.

I will set you free like the waves in the ocean that caress the sea with
their rhythm and motion. Waves that come in unison, combing the sand
as they come to rest.

I will set you free like a butterfly who just got its wings, adorned by
beautiful colors, a splendor for anyone to see.

I will set you free, wishing always that you can come back to me one day
and share your love as I always wished it could have been. I set you free,
my love, and let you go. But my love will be with you forever because
my heart you took with you in your departure.

Why Did We Have to End…?

Ending something when it had just started, we had only just begun to really be acquainted with each other.

It's like stepping on a sand castle once it's finished.

It's like breaking an egg once it has started hatching.

It's like opening a flower bud as it has just displayed itself.

It's like so many picturesque things in their initial stage. We needed time apart in order to grow … we are not suppose to end this way … there are still so many things unsaid, so many things not yet done, so many moments to share, so many times to spend with each other.

It makes no sense! Don't let it end! Please, darling, don't give up on us! Just try a little harder, push yourself stronger, be a little braver, and just call me up someday.

I will be waiting for you and I will greet you with open arms because my heart still beats for you…. So get a move on, loosen up your mind, don't fight it, please don't give up.

Don't be so full of pride; it won't be so hard. Just be humble and everything you want, you will be worthy of.

Today I Just Discovered

Today I just discovered what a liar a man can be
Instead of being honest and stating what they feel
A man will go in circles to avoid saying what's real

Cover up a lie with another lie as if others can't tell
Make up a fabulous story to hide away the reality
Promise to call you but never seems to respond
You lie about our friendship; you lie about you
You lie to keep me hoping and left an open door
Of questions never answered

Leaving open the wound you caused by your rebuff
You think I am a fool? That I can't tell you're playing mind games?
And who's to win at this? I could answer that it's neither you nor me at
best
No matter how good you play, no matter how sweet the lies,
No matter how competitive you really are, it isn't going to help this time
For you lost out on this game and no re-match is bound

For you lost out on a friendship and lost out on my love as well
I trusted you with all my heart; and senseless enough shared with
You so many things I wasn't supposed to tell!
You betrayed my trust and showed you never cared
For how was I to know that you were never there?

That you pretended to listen, and I thought you really cared
I believed in you, trusted you, and thought you were so different
But now I know you was not really who I thought you were
A friend I thought I found. But a friend keeps all his promises
And doesn't betray the trust, the trust that I had given you

I have not asked for much. I have not wanted from you what you could
not
Either give nor did I expect to have you love me
This is not me! I only wanted an answer
This is all, can't you see? No need to lie more
I see right through you. No need to tell me anything
Your silence has said it all!

Claribel Coreano

You ignore me if you want! It's you who will have to face the facts one
day
I know now that it has all been a lie
A lie to a friend

Excuses, Lies, and Deception

Excuses, lies, and deception make up the hypocrisy of a person
Make excuses for everything you do not want to do or could do
I cannot be with you because you are too serious
An excuse
I cannot help you right now because I am too busy
An excuse
I cannot make it this year to see you
An excuse
I cannot change my character
An excuse
I cannot stop what I know is hurting me
An excuse
You soon will be comfortable with excusing yourself from everything

Tell a lie one time, it becomes so easy to repeat habitually
One lie becomes two lies; before you know it your life is full of lies
I am faithful
Lies
I am a good soul at heart
Lies
I am a responsible man
Lies
I am a good listener and communicator
Lies
Your lies dictate the pretentious life you live
Your lies are so good that you believe they're true
The lies you tell and believe keep you living in a daydream

Deception is the word of the day
Deception only makes you look like a fool
Deception by hiding the truth
Deception by telling lies
Deception for not being yourself
Deception for being someone else
Deception for lying to your heart and mind

How long do you think the deception can continue?
How long do you think lies can last without the truth coming out?
How long do you think your excuses can be forgiven?
How long do you think you can pretend to be someone you are not?

The syndrome is **E.L.D.**
Excuses, Lies, and Deception
Unfortunate disease of a selfish person

Substitute Love

You substitute my love for the love of another
Who might be beautiful in features but has a heart that's a liar!
She might be shaped like an angel, but that's just the devil in disguise.
She might be a smooth talker, for that is all she knows how to do.
She was able to convince you and robbed you away,
And if you are smart enough you will ask around and see if she is really real.
You might soon find out that you haven't been the first one
She has said, "I love you, I will be 'faithful,'" to!
Yes, she has those qualities and a heart as black as coal, for in her heart there is
No remorse for stealing someone's love!

Everything I Can

I think that I have done my part by being patient
I have done everything I can
Still he does not make up his mind and continues to debate with heart
and mind
I have maintained myself faithfully for somebody who does not even
appreciate me
I often ask myself is it really love I feel?
My soul answers me back
It is deeper than you believe and perceive!

For I am past that stage of romance
I am in the part of life of reality and accepted wisdom
Thoughts of how wonderful it will be to share my dreams with him
The one who owns my heart and mind

I've become conscious that he is the one
He is the one I want to spend the rest of my life with
For real love is not that stage of "being in love"
It is an action, a decision to pass to the next level
You will know when you pass the obstacle course
Questioning myself, "Is he the one I want to love for the rest of my life?"
The answer in my heart is clear and in my mind a resounding yes is
declared!
Yes, I love him even though he does not know it nor will he ever
acknowledge it

I pray each day that he can realize it and meet me where I am
And accept me, heart to heart
Envision our life together and learn to share his life with me
But I often have a worry that one day it will be too late
I keep waiting and waiting
And he never comes my way

One day I will be strong enough to tell him
You lost out; someone else has come around
My heart has been won by a brave man
Who did not fear life itself
Answers he provided instead

Told me what I wanted to hear
A commitment we discussed
To share our lives without any apprehension
I realized that in life you do not need to love
You can learn to get adjusted
Share with them out of respect as long as they treat you well
You will then learn to love them

No Time Left to Rekindle

You looked at me and said, "How foolish have I been, mistreating you,"
When all you ever wanted to do was to love me.
I yearn to touch you and be by your side;
I miss your love and I want to come home again.
You think to yourself and say, "How ignorant have I been;
I have taken advantage of a pure and innocent love. Now her love for me
is gone."
There is no time left for me to rekindle her love. What can I do? I want to
try and save what's left or at least try to pick up the pieces of her broken
heart."
I look at you and say, "Remember when it was I who cried for your love?
I cried out for you to love me and change your ways, and make me a
happy woman." But I guess that wasn't enough to make you think and to
make you realize what you have done.
Honey, I think now it is too late for changes. Don't try to rekindle a love
that's gone. You see, my heart belongs to someone else,
someone special that makes me feels like a total woman.
He has shown me so many things in such a short time
This would have taken you a lifetime to accomplish.
Don't you think it is too late now for you to try and rekindle my love?
For my clock ran out of time …
and there is no turning back the hands of time….

I Wish I Had Never Met You!

I

I would have wished never to have known you or have had you cross my path.
If I would had never known you, I would have never fallen in love.
If I would have never known the sound of your voice and the way it touched my heart,
I would not have ever discovered how our souls were once connected.
I would have never known that you and I were destined.
I know now that it was not the right time, the right moment.
Nor were you ready to accept or believe that what happened between us was meant to be.
It is too painful, knowing that what I saw in you you never did see in me.
I would have preferred not to have known that you ever existed: no name, no face, no memories;
To know that my heart belongs to you without any effort on my part.
I fell in love with you, not knowing how and when it began
Or the what and why it happened to me.
At the moment in which it did, I was not looking to fall in love.
My heart was set on meeting a friend whom I could talk to
And who would just basically listen to me.
I was looking to have just a moment in time where
I as a single woman could stride along with no one to deride,
The fact that I have gained my freedom from a very sad past,
To know that you light up a path where I can see the many beautiful things.

II

I saw in your own heart.
I know this is real love because I am willing to let go.
I send this love to heaven to be guarded by the angels,
To be kept safe and held until your time to love is set,
So that when you find it in whomever, I don't know,
I know it will touch your soul and you will know
What it is to find true love
And you will finally in your life experience what I once had to endure.
You will remember me and your heart will know that this is my love
You found, which you lost long ago.
I gave it as a gift to you for all the cherished moments,

Although so briefly I still feel like I have known you forever.
I appreciate every conversation, every phone call, and every connection
we've made.
This will always stay in my heart forever, and I will miss you for the rest
of my life
But I am not selfish; I wish that in your life you find happiness
And all the good things you deserve, because I know you are a good
man.
It's mind boggling how I can see the goodness in your heart,
How much I admired the very fine man you are.
I know you deserve the best and I wish with every tear that falls
Much happiness, love, and success.
Life experience is a learning tool to help us grow and make us strong.
A lesson which I have learned is that what we want at times
Is not yet for us,
That there is always a right time, moment, and right place to find all that
is lost.
I, however, will never know how it feels to be with the one I love.

My Heart is Broken

My heart is broken, in many pieces
Pain so deep it feels like a stabbing knife
Wounds unhealed
Words unsaid
Questions unanswered
What a mistake
Gave all of my heart in a moment
Loved you instantly
Did not think this could happen to me
Scared me quickly
Afraid of the feelings I was feeling
Did not want to love you
Was not expecting it
Could not stop it
Tried to forget you but I can't
Tried so hard to remove you from my mind
Endless effort but in vain
I ended up crying tears of missing you instead
Cannot explain why me? Why me?
He does not even answer
No clue has he of what I truly feel in my heart and mind
I am being tortured by his rejection
Hurts so bad
Pain so deep
Could not time heal me please?
Forgive and forget, I tried that already
What you do not see cannot hurt you
Why am I being haunted by his presence?
Missing him so much
Like the love of my life has died
Could not imagine such an emotion
To love so deeply
To know him so well
To feel and sense his isolation
To sense when something is going wrong
I feel his sadness sometimes during the night
I often feel anxious not knowing
What to do with this connection

Part of my soul is missing
Part of me has died....

My mind is tortured
By the memories
Of the times we shared together
No doubts had I when we were close
No fears or distractions
My hope and love I share with you those days
Felt so great to talk for hours
Hear you laugh
See you serious
Playing your guitar
I enjoyed so much
Just a calm way of being
You and I peacefully enjoying each other's company
The comfort level was there
The trust as well
The flaws I accepted
Saw beyond your soul
A great future for us
Share some dreams, exchanged some goals
We could be just great partners
We are a good team together
However, fear got in the way
Pride built a wall between us
Selfishness separated us
Unrealistic expectations
You were for the moment
I was forever
You were for the past time
I was for keeps
You were for pleasure
I was for love
You were for the romance
I was for companionship
You did not believe
You did not accept
You did not want
What I hope
What I have faith for

What I know could have been a great relationship
You wanted many more to enjoy
I wanted just you
I feel that we are both so miserable without each other
No matter how hard we both try to pretend
No matter how much you ignore me
I know you miss me as well
No matter how much you think that I am not what you seek
I know that I am that and more
No matter how hard you tried to convince yourself
That I was just a good time for the moment
I know that I was the best woman you had ever had
Could not handle so much love
I even remember that day in the summer in the Keys
What I thought was so romantic
A candlelight dinner
Wine, flowers
Love in my heart for you
You rejected out of fear
Never been loved so naturally
I did not feel rejected that day
I only felt your fear
I did not question the why
I knew the reasons
I did it from my heart and mind
Did not matter to me
I quietly let you be
No need to feel any pressure
I was just being me
A loving soul who gives without any inhibitions
I still enjoyed my dinner that day
Nevertheless, I knew you were scared
To be loved
Cared for
Pampered
And shown so much love
That it scared you....
I knew then I must go
Leave and let go
It is not fair for me to love for the both of us
Unconditionally I love you

However, who knows where your heart and mind are now?
You have not voiced a sound
Silence is fear
Truth to voice what you feel
Freedom is to express your feelings
Yes, my heart is broken and my mind is tormented
That does not change my feelings for you a bit

No Looking Back

I

No looking back at the past, for it has long been forgotten
No need to relive the bad memories as they have happened
Release it, and learn from your mistakes
Get stronger to know that you are smarter now
No one or nothing can cause you any pain

No looking back at the mistakes you've made
Don't keep track of all the wrongs that have been made
Just make believe that an imaginary eraser
Has finally made everything fade away

No looking back to those lovers from the past
No need to ever remember
Their selfish ways
Forget that they one day existed
Just remember, don't repeat the same mistakes again

Don't ever look back—look towards the present
For no one knows what the future may have
Every day is a bright new day to start life fresh
Breathe the air that makes us alive
Give thanks for every breath in spite
For life is too precious to waste any time

Regretting things that you thought you might want to have
Material things are perishable, people come and people go
Friends here, friends there, no one stays for very long
Husbands leave, wives disappear
Lovers come and lovers go
No one ever stays for long....

Money is also temporary; the more you have the more you want
Fame and fortune are just a title deep down inside
We are all alike: one heart, one spirit, and one soul
What makes you happy can make someone else cry
What you consider good someone else might think is bad
Accept that we are all different on the outside

But inside the anatomy is the same and has the same impressions in an
x-ray

II

Remember the times you laughed instead; forget the times you shed a
tear
For we all suffer, never fear
No one can say, "I love being alone," for everyone needs a shoulder to
lean on
Never say, "Love doesn't exists"; it really does. You might just be too
blind to see
For one day when it was staring you in your face, you let it go
For being proud, too stubborn to admit this could be it
Let me give it a chance and then you will see
For anyone in life can pretend to be
Pretend to be something they think
But it is really not their own self they see
It is just someone pretending to be me

Look in the mirror at a closer view
Are you happy with what you see?
Are you real in every way
Or do you carry a suitcase with a different face
So no one knows which one is the real you?

You feel great around your friends; you share their success instead
Have time for everyone around you, with the exception of the little angel
Who waits behind you for a view
And someone who cares deeply about you
Who patiently waits behind the scenes

When will you learn to stop and cherish the things
That really matter?
Soon enough time will go faster than you could ever imagine
You will be replaced with all of those things that you think matter
Left with no energy you seek, those you shun away
Little angel grew up like a princess
When are you coming by, "Dad"?
"I don't know but I'll see you soon!"

Remember those very same words will be told again
For history will repeat itself
And your daughter will say the same to you one day

Don't think life just centers around you only; remember Howard Hughes
He felt the world was his to be known and he spent his life all alone
For money, women, drugs, and pleasure
Were his only ambition
Died a horrible death all alone on his bed
No one there to claim him and say, "Hey, I once loved this man"

The Dialogue of Middle-Age Crisis

ME: I have accepted that you do not care for me
Or feel any interest towards me
Your silence has said it all
But the truth be told
My life is like an open book
Live in truth, never lie
Don't need to impress
For what?
I am me! I love me!
Your rejection, I brushed it off my shoulder
I live to learn, learn to live
No looking back please....

YOU: I have told myself she is not what I seek
She is not what I desire
She is not young and virile
She is a mature woman in her forties
She is so sure of what she wants out of life
She knows exactly what she accepts and denies
She doesn't think twice about who is right or wrong
She sees things differently all along
Her heart is pure and simple
Her love for me is too much for me to handle
She is trustworthy and true to me
Although I don't deserve it
Loves me unconditionally without me earning her love
She waits patiently for me to return
Like a sweet memory of dreams gone by
Wind softly blowing along her side
The shadow of her sweetness and caresses I can't forget
Relived the memories of her sweet scent....
She loved me like no other
She gave like no other gave
Her love for me I felt that day
But I in my stubbornness I denied it till today
The mature woman who caressed my body
From head to toe
Until my body quivered in ecstasy

Her warmth and energy I sense
My heart and mind very at ease
A longing she felt for me like no other
In her hands I felt the energy
Of a woman who is completely sure of herself
And knew that the moment was to be ours forever
She knew that it was I who would steal her heart
And leave it broken in pieces
Without any mending or remedy
Just the silence of my fear
Pridefulness of my character
That this beautiful woman who gave all to me that day
Was not the one I thought I wanted?

YOU:
I have stated that I want a younger woman
Young spirit, mind, and body
I hope to relinquished
A trophy wife to model
Feel young every day as long as I am with her
You think to yourself, "Being in my forties myself, I think I can last forever"

ME: My darling, I think that you are so confused
I saw this before a long time ago, that you still hold onto younger years
Like a child who fears to grow old gracefully
I knew that you would seek a younger woman; I think I did tell you that one day
In the kitchen of your apartment as we cooked
Your smirk and smile gave you away
If you remember that I left you and gave you your space
For you to wonder and search for your prize
Did not want to stand in your way, no way
I knew that you did not see things my way
A wise woman who accepted that leaving the love of my life
Sacrifice it in order that you might find yourself and your happiness
Wise in years make no mistakes
I know that I was your soul mate
But what a shame it has been that you did not have the courage
To stay, seek me, search, and communicate
Find out things

And then you would have seen that I am as young
As your heart desired
Free-spirited
Fun-willed mind
But a woman my age you do not want
You have said that I am set in my ways
But may I ask what they are? You cannot be so sure of yourself
For you are as old as me; what can I say? The benefit will be for a short time
The lies will outlive the happiness
The beauty is only skin deep
The young mind and spirit
Can turn dark and wicked
Leaving you in despair
Pain from her trickery
Then you will think and relive my pain
Acknowledge that it was just a mid-life crisis …
That the memories would have been so much sweeter
And love would have lasted so much longer
If only you would have considered the love
From this forty-year-old woman
Bittersweet … Regrets that you will not forget

It's Your Loss Not Mine

I

It's your loss not mine; you can ignore me if you want
Who cares anymore? It's your game not mine
What you gain I don't know
Can't reach out and be honest
Why do you have to be so cold hearted?
Speak up, say what's up
Don't play games
There is no time
I am hanging on by a thread
Either let me go
Cut me loose
Or break away
But please tell me why!

I deserve some answers
I deserve the truth
I need to keep on with my life
Tell me what went wrong
Tell me where we failed
But don't leave me hanging on
Hanging by a thread
Don't you communicate with your business partners?
You never leave questions unanswered
So what is wrong with letting me know?
I could have been your life partner

I need to know to be able to be stronger
To learn how to deal with the situation
If that is the case and we are a mistake
Let me know. I'm running out of time
Don't you know that you will one day
Be in the same predicament as mine.
In love with someone
Who does not have the time.
Ignored you as much as you have ignored me.
For the world is round
What is here today
Tomorrow is the other way around

II

Listen here; give me some answers
I need to have the peace of mind
The peace to keep on going
Going without you …
The closure so I can let go
And find my way back within

So many times you talked about trust
And spirituality you always discussed
But you don't practice what you preach
Honesty in friendship, that's the key to open doors
Learn to give to others so in life you could have more

What are you afraid of?
What are you trying to prove?
That your intellect is higher?
Honey, I wasn't trying to dispute that
Your status or your title
Is that what makes you feel secure?
What happens if you don't have that
Then where will you be obscure?

Be clear, show some respect
Don't hide, come out and show your face
For I gave you my respect as another human being would
If not, what planet do you come from?
If you cannot acknowledge me
Let's not pretend anymore
That this is yet another of your games
Stop it already; you are a man
Grow up; come out of the shell

Stop thinking that you are a teenager—
Those days are long gone
You are entering another stage in life
And soon you will be old
Let me ask you this
Do you intend to live alone for the rest of your life
Just because you are too proud

Too proud to share and care?
For a friend who tried somehow to let you know
That love is the only way, the only way the world goes around

You'd Rather Lose Me

You'd rather go on in life without me
Because you are too proud to see that you love me
Too stubborn to see the truth
Too selfish to want to share with me
I guess you are waiting for someone exactly like you
Who will take you for granted
Use you and then discard you
And not even say "good-bye"
For this person will have the same purpose as you
You will think that she is the one
And say, "I will make her my wife"
But when you do, you will see
She is just the spitting imagine of you
You will be looking dead at yourself
No mirror to reflect
For you finally found your reflection
But would you like to be staring at "yourself" constantly
Thinking why me? Why me?
See, in life you don't need an equal but a balance
Of chemistry, for it will become too boring to be with yourself 24/7
Remember what you wish for can come true
But might not be beneficial to you
For instead of having a partner next to you
Your enemy may be by your side
Remember, in life there is always an evil twin
So having someone just like you might not be agreeable
Instead, look for the balance that can teach you how to love
A caring heart , a calm soul, and gentle spirit
Don't ignore
Someone who really knows how to care and understand
When you are in crisis, provide you some guidance
And wisdom to let you grow spiritually
I will be your guiding light, shine on your path to see the road
Hold your hand when you are afraid
Embrace you when you are in fear
Pray for you when you lose all faith
Be right there for you instead
I will be the shoulder to lean on
For I am your partner, friend, and companion for life

R.I.P

Here lies my love for thee.
I will bury it at sea, for it has to die!
I bury it because I have no more tears to cry
Of unexpected causes;
I believe a "broken heart."
I waited in solitude for the man who never came to claim it.
Painful and deep the pain caused by the love of my life,
Who will never in his lifetime know of this innocent love
I have felt deep within my spirit.
I will bury it at sea, and the waves will take with it
The clear sound of his contagious laughter,
The piercing sound of his voice,
And the reflection of those dreaming eyes that haunt me day and night.

As farther away out to sea, I leave his future goals
And dreams he once had shared with me.
I hope they all do one day come true.
My wish for him I will set free with every blow of the wind,
That in his life he experiences what he has set out to be.
I will keep a faint picture in my mind of that fisherman on a boat
Casting his reel, preparing his hook and sinker with a self-satisfied smile,
Waiting patiently and proudly to catch a bigger, better dream.
And as the sun slowly dies down and the night skies set in
I promise to every star I see
I will forget this dark and handsome stranger
Whose life has impacted me.
I lay my heart to rest in peace and to be buried at sea.

I Set My Heart Free

I

I know that I must set you free,
Set you free to venture into your own daydream.
You have your fantasies and ideas.
To you, your ambitions are realistic
But to me, you are a dreamer
Who is wasting his best years on unfulfilled childish issues.
Why not save time to be spent with someone who will love you?

Nothing can change your way of thinking.
No one or thing can make you change your mind.
Your mind is set and your character is hard to break,
For you are used to your own ways.
Why think you need love to survive?
You're used to not having it at all.
I must set you free
And stand aside.

I have made up my mind.
I will not stand in your path,
For your thinking tells you
That I am just an
Obstacle in your direction.
The route is now clear
For you to venture out.

For you are used to not sharing.
Love for you comes in the form of disposable persons.
When you are done with them
You just get rid of them.
For you cannot stand
Having someone too long by your side.
It's as if you are afraid
That they will find out
Who you really are.

But you see, I have recognized long ago
Who you really are inside.
I knew about you before
You got the chance to say hi.
I did not run, afraid, nor did I judge you,
And I did stay.

II

I know you like a book, so I thought I would mention that...
I know the basis of your inspirations.
I know what triggers your desperation.
I know your anxieties; I know your fears.
And I know that your life is not yet clear.

You talk so profoundly about spiritual growth
But yet you ignore what path you should go forward on.
You have hardened your heart, you have deaf ears,
And your heart would not accept
The path that God has in store for you.

For you are holding onto your younger years,
Fearing maturity
Like a child in fear,
Hiding in darkness
Away from the light,
Thinking no one will find you
Nor see you in sight.

But just remember no matter how far you try to run,
No matter how far you plan to go,
No matter how dark the place you be in,
Remember that God sees everything
And nothing is hiding from
his sight and from His will.

Keep in mind, my friend and love of my life,
That the years go by silently and rapidly.
So far, no one has been able to stop death.
The energy that you still have left
Do not waste on things from this earth.

The flicker of light that still shines in your heart,
Don't let it die but let it shine for the love of God.
With tears in my eyes, I beg you to think,
To re-think of the real meaning of life,
To think of the reasons I crossed your path,
To think that in life things don't just happen by error
But that there is a greater purpose for you to see,
That God is still waiting for you.

III

My only hope in life for you, my love, is
That your heart will be touched
And that you can see the clarity.
Reconsider your existence.
Search your soul for the real reasons.
Think in your mind of the purpose.
God has even used individuals to share His love with you

There are not too many people whom God uses
To send you a message expressly for your soul,
So personal and confidential
That He has taken the time to tell you
That you need Him and that your life will be finally complete
Once you accept His will.

You will not regret it.
You will finally see,
What my heart has witnessed.
You will find true happiness
And real purpose in life.
You will be thankful
That you were set free
From a life of wrongdoing.

God will break all the chains and bondages
That you struggle with every day and the heart of
God will heal your heart from the past transgressions of pain.
God will heal your broken spirit
And show you hope
And the love you have been waiting for all along.

My love, I will never give up on you.
And even though I will not be by your side,
You will always be in my heart
And I will pray each day that you can find
The joy of God and His truth.
For I know that we are not a mistake
But an enlightenment of two souls
Who needed each other to grow spiritually.

Spiritual Journey
Part I Life's Meaning

In My Life

I

In my life I have been blessed to meet many individuals whose lives have impacted me. I have been able to interact with all kinds of people; some rich, some very poor, some homeless, some mentally ill, some dying, some crooked, some criminal and lost in spirit. For in each and every one, I learned something that helped me to deal with my own issues and to see a clearer path.

Sometimes we take for granted the lessons to be learned, for in each human being there is a message or a sign of help. Only some have the ability to see past the human shield and see what the spirit is saying or crying for.

I've been able to attain so many beautiful experiences, to be able to reach out to others whose spirits have been broken, who have lost all hope in life, and who do not see any light. I have been blessed by God and given wisdom to say a comforting word or suggestion that can light a small candle and help them see the road.

It's amazing how many beautiful people God has used to speak to me and to reach out to my spirit and let me see the plans that He has for me. I never in my life wanted to heed the call, but now I am older and understand the purpose of my life. I did, however, meet someone who has a special calling but does not want to heed His call; he does not know how special he is in God's eyes to be so fortunate to be called to do His work.

I lost him as a friend; my soul mate he was, but he does not believe it and refuses to accept it. Our separate ways we went; no calls, no hellos, not even a good-bye, for his pride and arrogance got in our way. Too proud to believe that I could be the one, too arrogant to accept that he and I were one. A team that was meant to be, companions like childhood friends, two lovers who were blessed to find that our souls connected and we were meant to be.

II

How sad it has been for me to lose my best friend. He does not understand that in life things happen the way God wants them to, not the way we write them down on a to-do list. Things that we want, we don't always get: the fame, the money, the fortune. God knows how we would behave if we did have them; he knows that these things might not be beneficial to our spirit, and lost in darkness we will become.

For too much of a good thing is wrong; remember what you are seeking might not be the thing you need, and what you are planning might not be the plan He has for you. What you are wishing for might not be convenient but sometimes He has allowed us to get them against His will. When this happens, He stands outside the picture, for he cannot deal in darkness until we learn our lesson and break free. See the light and humble ourselves from our sins and His Holy Spirit comes back to guide and show us the way.

My friend, my love, how I wish that I could make you understand that it is in God that we find happiness and become so rich with joy that nothing this world brings can make up for this feeling. I sincerely can say that I love you so much not to give up praying for you, even if you are not with me; I know that one day my heart will be overjoyed when you are saved. That would be the happiest day of my life because I know that I will be able to see my best friend and soul mate in heaven.

To write it down on paper seems so simple and comes so easily; to tell you in person seems so hard and difficult. For you see, I believe and you do not; therefore, a shadow stands between us. I believe in God first, I believe in us, and I believe in you. No matter how distant you become, my prayers will be with you, and with all my soul I will pray that you can get closer to God. For this is my sincerest wish this Christmas to God, that my best friend can finally find out that God is the only way. Faith is my only friend at this point, and hope my companion, for I lost the most important person in my life. I question it at times, but I understand that this is something I must do, and that is to let go ... and let God.

My Life Journey

I

All my life I have often wondered what has been the purpose of my life

My journey has been difficult. I've been through struggles unimaginable

And it's hard to comprehend; I myself have a hard time accepting

All the ups and downs my journey has exposed me to

Often in solitude I cried and prayed to God for answers

I have asked God for wisdom and understanding

But instead I have encountered trials and tribulation

Indeed I have been taught a hard lesson in life

Because from my mistakes, I acquired knowledge about the good and the bad

At forty years old, I now know I have to accept my life journey

And that everything I have been through have been gainful experiences

Which have led me to knowledge and wisdom in a very thorny route

Even though the trials and tribulations have been challenging

I know that God has been by my side

I hear His voice telling me, "My child I will never leave your side"

A blueprint plan I have for you, if only you would have focus"

But in my ignorance I did the opposite and continued to do things in my style

How long did it take for me to finally see?

II

Life would have gone much smoother if only I had listened to His voice

But now that I am older I understand that

He is the one to follow; there is no other way

On a life journey, what counts is that we grow spiritually

To prepare us for a better place

And even though I am a sinner

I know that I will be saved

For who's to judge me for the way I have lived my life?

And like Jesus said, "Who will throw the first stone?" for we all are sinners

No one is protected but a loving heart God sees, and not my mistakes

For what greater mercy than to have God's love instead?

I did not get a chance to find that unconditional love in a man

Neither success, nor wealth, nor education, nor fame, nor popularity,

Nor intellectuality, nor material things can bring about happiness

But what is necessary to make peace within ourselves

and refuge within the Creator up above?

I accept that I am preparing for a better destination

Where my troubles, heartaches, pain, and mistakes

Will not even exist, but the peace and tranquility

III
Of God's comfort and security.

There I will be someone important and be special to him

I will be compensated for the wisdom

That I have shared with others in this world

Whose journey has been unpleasant. To a great extent

I will rejoice now in the Lord, for my time here is short

I know that I will soon be going to a better place

No more painful times for me

For I have gained enough experience on my journey

That I am ready to meet my Creator

I accept that he is calling me

And I know that I must heed the call

No call-waiting or on hold or leave a message

Or beep me when you are ready

God wants the answer to the call

I must tell him!

"Yes, Lord Jesus,

Come and get me when I am ready—I am ready to go home"

The Purpose of My Life

Lord, I did not know until now that there is a purpose for my life.
I was just living in uncertainty from one day to the next,
Not knowing where to go, how to seek, or where it could be found.
I lived each day feeling an empty space inside my heart,
Looking for things to fill it but never ever satisfied.

I went the wrong way as a young woman, took many turns, and failed in
life.
Every time I went down, I got back up again with hope that a miracle
would come about,
Struggled again to find the answers, looked for spirituality,
Self-help books, but nothing did the trick.
I went on living my routine; looking to fill the void, I
Tried many things again. It did not work
Until one day on the spur of the moment I packed my bags
And left my past behind in Bridgeport,
Took off driving to another place
until I reached my destination in Florida, paradise of a place.
The Lord called me to a church, and that very same day
He spoke to me and said, "It's not a mistake you are here.
God has a plan for your life; He brought you here for a purpose."
Renewal is what I called it,
Reborn is how I feel, no longer bound to sin.
Not feeling lost and in darkness,
I now see the day is clear.
The Lord has changed my attitude.
The Lord has changed my belief.
The Lord has given me hope.
With His grace He has saved my soul.
Salvation is the answer for all who seem lost.
Salvation is the answer for your heart-empty void.
Direction He can give you,
Provide you with a plan.
The Holy Spirit will guide you
And show you many miracles in your life.

Joy and comfort you will feel even when you are experiencing sorrow.
A new lease in life I have,
A new vision I see;
That the love I needed was always in front of me
And the Lord has watched over me.
And patiently waited for me to accept the offer of salvation.
I have been redeemed, washed by the blood of the Lamb.
A new creation I am in Christ.
A new me and a new way of doing things.
I am no longer weak.
I am strong, for He gives me strength.

I feel that the best thing I have ever done in my life has been to be saved.
Thank you, Lord, for saving my soul and giving your love in place of it.
For nothing in this world matters if you are not the center of it.
It's meaningless to live without God in your heart.
It's like being in outer space, simply a flying star.
No boundaries, no light, no beginning or end,
Just wandering in darkness with no purpose
Or guidance.
This is what being lost in sin can be.
Open your heart.
Hear His voice.
Let Him in.
He will remove the past.
He will cleanse your soul.
He will change your way of thinking.
He will heal your heart.
He will make you new.
He will show you the plans He set for your life long before you were
born.
He knew you even before the beginning of time
So why hide from Him?
Why shun His love?
Why ignore Him?
Why lose your soul...?
He loves you so,
Waits for your return.

Is It Worth It?

Is it worth it? To keep struggling?
To keep up with the crowd?
Is it worth it? Trying to keep up with the lies?
Is it worth it? Being something you are not?
Is it you? Or is it someone else?
Do you know if you please you or everyone else?
Making others happy is your façade
Struggling hard to be like them
Trying hard to fit into someone else's shoes
Forfeit who you were meant to be
Risk life, originality for some unrealistic schemes
Trying to fit in into someone else's way of life
Assimilating to be like them
Hate yourself so much that it seems tainted
To be truly who you really are
Hide in shame
Hide in fear
Hide in silence
Hide away from being real
Why lose who you are?
Why not keep your soul intact?
Love yourself enough
To love who you really are inside
Deep emotions hard to fight
Left you hanging in painful fright
Forging yourself and who you were to be
Why? Can you please tell me why?
When life could be so much simpler
Accepting yourself and your flaws
Loving you enough to choose between
What is wrong and what is right?
Why destroy that beautiful soul and spirit God gave you?
The chosen purpose for you to heed
The call to the real meaning of your life
The happiness that is not achieved through selfish means
Be who you are meant to be
Love with all your heart and soul
Healing then will begin

Accepting love
Not shunning it
Pleasure, pleasure soon your senses
Will become numb to it
Nothing will ever gratify
No comfort
No soothe
No peace
No satisfaction
Only relentless actions
Consequences for bad choices you will have to face
Hurt and pain you will experience again
Tears will fall from your eyes like rain
Sorrow felt in your heart
Wishing back to have made the change
Only you and you only
Can retrieve the memories of the past
Only you and you only
Can remove the hurt from your heart
Only you and you only
Can make amends with all who hurt you
Only you and you only
Can make peace with your enemies
Only you and you only
Can realize the peace and tranquility
Simple cure
Through forgiveness
Resentments, vindications, and past, unresolved issues
Can destroy the faith to change
The hope to heal
The power of love
The energy to seek well
The trust in God
The humbleness of spirit
Gentleness of a good soul
Leave those things behind
Learn to trust in God
How can I make you understand?
That it is through Him and only Him
That we find the answers to peace
The power to heal

The blessing of grace?
God is love but judge's sin
He waits for your repentance
And for you to decide to do His will
How hard can that be?
To gain salvation
And lose worldly attention?

Winter 2003

In my aloneness I have found out that I am the only friend I have
No one comes around any longer, nor calls to say how are you? Are you
fine?
No family takes out the time to say, "Hey, we miss you" and "Wish you
were here"
At this moment I feel like I was born in the wrong family
Or that maybe I just don't fit in with them anymore
For I am just a poor woman with nothing to show
Lately in my life I have nothing significant
And my financial situation is difficult

For I am the lonesome dove of winter, outside in the cold
I feel the brisk, cold wind hitting me in my face
The wind so fiercely piercing in frozen breaths, my cheeks burn
I walk in the snow of the cold winter without a coat or warm air
That's how my heart feels at this moment: desolate
Knowing that I don't matter much to anyone anymore
In the solitude that life has exposed me to
Sadness strikes me without warning
Just a reminder of where I came from
And the struggles that in my life I've had to face.

Four decades have passed and in my life I have gone through so many
changes
I lived the stage of not caring about anything
When I was younger, for I felt that I was indispensable
So young that the future did not matter
For living with no cares makes you so reckless
Not thinking of what was right or what was wrong
I just lived life as it took place

When life allowed me to be a wife, I took it seriously
And was the best wife one could have
I dedicated myself to the role of spouse and mother all life long
Cared for children and managed a home
Took out the time to care for a husband as well
But who cared for me? No one did at all!
Faithful always, that was me; committed to the marriage that was keen

But what for? What did it bring me?
I lived many years without his attention or a kind word coming out of his
mouth
I was as alone, alone as a mouse in a big house
No one ever told me that life was not supposed to be like that
I was too naïve to understand why
All I saw was that I had to work at it without a worry
That was just a stage of life that I was in

Late in my thirties I realized that life can't be wasted
And that I should not stay with someone whose mind, soul, and spirit
Are not there, but an empty soul with walls to stare
The husband I thought was my husband
Was just a stranger in my house
I did not know who he really was, for he never shared anything sacred
with me
He was just a roommate who lived a double life
For he gave the best of himself to other women who knew him better than
I did
Life got dangerous during these times and I had to break free from living
a lie
Before I knew it, the truth came out, and pictures tell a thousand stories
Finally his deception came to light and the truth found out was my key to
freedom
Yes, it hurt! A woman scorned, humiliated, and mistreated
I am only a fragile crystal rose that shattered on the floor
From all the pressures and mishandling of life itself, it did not matter to
me anymore

A few years have passed and I have been reborn; I came back to life
again
For I found out that Jesus was my only friend
And that in life I had to learn. Learn to trust only in him
The lessons I have experienced I can say have taught me to become a
wiser woman
I no longer feel the shame or the sadness of being betrayed
For my best friend Jesus, He suffered more
He was betrayed in the weakest stage of His life
And nailed to a cross with no one there to set Him free
He did it all because he cared for me

He was mocked, beaten, scorned, and insulted
There he remained in solitude on the Calvary
At the foot of the cross with his arms open, waiting for death, alone He
stood
A sacrifice unimaginable to all
He stood in awe and saved us all
By His grace I found salvation
By his sacrifice I found an inspiration
By His love I found hope
Through his care I obtain faith
That I am a new creation
I have found the answers to my life
I have been reborn into a different woman
My life is just beginning
My happiness comes from inside
And I no longer feel alone, for He is next to me all day long
Every day, every night, years come and years go
And He still remains the same
The redeemer who rescued me
From living a life in hell

From the Darkness

From the darkness into the light
I was blind and now I see
Dwelling in a sea of sin
I could not even swim to shore
Trying to find peace in material things
Trying to find love in all the wrong places
Trying to find acceptance
Trying to find serenity
What a mistake of me
How much time did I waste on selfish things
Thinking that having possessions will make me happy?
Thinking love is a feeling not an action?
Thinking recognition comes from others?
Fighting hard for my peace of mind?
Trying to reach harmony with worldly things?
I now know how lost I was

I found the answer to my problems
I found the one who supplies for me even without asking
I found the love that it is unconditional
I found the peace and tranquility that only He can give

I found the most important being in this world
I found God on my way towards self-destruction
On the road there He stood waiting for me with open arms
Telling me there is still time; come and follow me
The light of His spirit has shown me to trust in Him only
My heart, soul, and mind I gave Him instead
He is Lord of my life
He has changed my tears to joy
He has given me a new beginning in life
He has blessed me with hope
My spirit understands now what I was seeking
That serenity that only the Lord gives us
No drink, no highs, no man, no money
Can even come close to this feeling
The most amazing love I have found in Him
Thank you, Lord, for saving me
But a miracle I still await that my friend can find you as well

Spiritual Journey
Part II My Hope and Faith Lies in the Lord

Waiting For a Miracle

I cry alone in silence; my soul is weary from trying
Trials and tribulations have made me doubt my own existence
My pain and sorrow have been too hard for me
I tried to handle it, to face it and fix it
But it has been rough; I have not yet been able to do it alone
I seek some relief, but I am unable to find it
I wait for a miracle even when hope seems dim
I still see a flicker of light that shines in
Giving me faith to keep on waiting
I will not give up and I will not deny my God
I will keep on praying, for this is my connection to the heavens
I know that sooner or later my God will lift me up
And He will deliver me from all life's mishaps
No matter how long it takes
I know that it is at the Lord's time, not mine
Wait for my Miracle, this is what I must do

I know my Savior will rescue me
He will bless me greatly
The renovation in my life will make me shine
Individuals will be amazed at the changes in my persona
I will be a testimony of truth guided in light
For the Lord will bless me with a new beginning
Others will know why I, a humble soul,
Was saved from this plight
And God's tender mercy has touched my spirit
Provided me with hope, faith, and charity: these are my new friends
Wisdom, understanding, and caring: these are gifts to be revealed
Humbleness, clarity, and reverence for life
That will be the new me
A kind word, a caring heart, a forgiving soul
And love to give to others
My vocation in life has changed; I have a new calling
I am going to do God's work instead
The miracle I await will not be just a wish anymore
For God will save my friend
His life will be new as well
For he will find a new beginning

And share his miracle with me one day
The miracle I await I know it soon will be done
For God hears the tears and the anguish of my afflicted heart
For I pray to Him with all my heart and soul

Rescue Me

Lord, sometimes I feel like I am drowning in a whirlpool;
Left with no breath I scream out please rescue me.
I have no will power left, no energy to fight.
I see only darkness in front of my eyes.
My soul is leaving my body, in front of my sight.
Please rescue me.

This burden I can no longer carry,
This load has become too heavy for my arms to hold.
I can't drag it, I can't pull it away, and I can't even lift it out.
In front of your feet, dear Lord, I leave it.
Have mercy and carry my burden of pain.
Jesus, you died for my sins and took all my fears, sins, and past away.
For every drop of blood that fell to the ground,
You washed my sins somehow.
For every pain you felt,
You suffered for me instead,
Carried the cross without complaint
As sweat came rolling down your face.
Tired and lonely that day you looked to the heavens and said,
"God, forgive them."
I thank you, Lord, for that sacrifice through grace.
You healed my dying soul
And with your last breath gave me life instead.
Lord, you rescued me from drowning, drowning in the sea of pain.

Hear Me, Lord

Hear me, Lord; I pray on my knees, waiting for justice
I cry for answers, I pray for a resolution
I beg for mercy and wait in silence
Lord, hear my anguish; my soul cries out for your comfort
A 911 call to heaven has been placed
Hear me out, Lord; my heart feels like it's in pieces
I ask how much more, Lord, can I undertake
Only you know how much I can endure in pain

Hear me, Lord, when I call out to you
Don't look at my mistakes
I know that I have made numerous errors,
Lord, that I have accepted
In all humbleness I have asked for you to save me
Have mercy on my soul
And give me a chance to be reborn

Lord, like Jacob fought with the angel for His blessings
I am also fighting for my blessing
With humbleness and reverence
I need your reassurance
I need the peacefulness of your Holy Spirit
I need a sign, Lord
I need a miracle
Lord, you say in your Word that if we ask in your name
We should receive
Lord, I believe in this promise
My faith and hope lies in you
That my life can change drastically
Because you have rescued me
All I need are some answers
All I need is your peace
All I need is your guidance
And this will set me free,
Lord, in all gratitude
I thank you for listening
For you are always there for me
Hear my soul cry out to you

Claribel Coreano

Please accept my humble prayer
Accept it as a gift
Like a butterfly that's been set free
I thank you, Lord, for hearing me....

Lord Make Me New

Lord, make me new, change my old habits into an optimistic view
Take from me all the pain and bad memories from my heart & mind
Erase from my heart any resentment that I may still have
Pull out any grudges that may still linger on

Make me free, Lord, I want to be a channel of peace
Lord, show me how to forgive my adversary
And those who have caused me intended harm
Let me say, "I forgive you, because the Lord has shown me how"

I know that I have to let go of various unhealthy emotions
For I am being reborn as an assertive woman of God
And I am no longer vulnerable or inactive
For you have set me free of my inner struggles

Take away my fears, teach me how to triumph over them
Let me be brave enough to try the things
I always wanted to undertake
And didn't because I was afraid
I no longer fear, Lord, for your Holy Spirit is near

I have a vocation to follow and I want to do your will
Lord, bless me enough to make the right choices
And guide me into the path you want me to follow

Lord, put love in my heart for others …
Wisdom and understanding to encourage
Humility and kindness to sympathize
To be wise in situations so that I do not appear weak
Be tamed like a dove, open minded to accept difficult situations
In touch with my feelings and emotions that I can gain reverence
Respect, honor, and have integrity to do your will

Let me not be judgmental in any circumstances
Lord, help me be fair and give the best of me
That I may encourage others to become the best they can be
Lord, I know you will bless me greatly
In return, Lord, I promise that I will share my blessings

With anyone I come in contact with
For I will be earnestly thankful throughout my lifetime
I will continuously express my sincerest gratitude

Lord, You Have Changed Me

Lord, you have come into my life and transformed my soul
I am not the woman I used to be; I am different
I have found the peace and joy that only you can give
I was lost in sin long ago, but now I have found a new life with you
Lord, you have forgiven my sins
You have forgiven my past
You have given me a dream
You have given me hope
Lord, I thank you for saving my soul

I never in my life would I have thought that this was all I needed
No one has provided the unconditional love you have given
No man has even come close to it
True joy comes from you, Lord

It is so amazing to know that the only way
In this world to gain true happiness
Is through you, Lord

I do not fret, Lord, because you are with me, for you have searched my
heart
Given me hope and a future
Lord, not even the leaves in a tree move without your consent
For every hair in my head, you have counted it
For you have known me since birth
The plans you have for me you have known all along

Lord, I trust in you, my faith is in you, and my spirit cries out to you,
Lord
For a miracle, for I know that nothing is impossible for you, Lord
Only you can transform a person
Only you can touch the heart of an individual
Only you can dig into the heart and search the soul
And spirit deep enough to make an individual see their sins
For your Word is living and active, sharp like a double-edged sword,
strong enough to Surpass the soul, spirit, and the mind
My only hope, Lord, is that one day my friend whom I care so deeply
about will be saved
I await a miracle and I do not lose hope, Lord

305

For I have confessed this miracle and I know that nothing is impossible
for you, Lord
If only he can see that the only true joy comes from you,
That only you can remove all that baggage from the past,
Only you can forgive his sins,
Only you can really make him see what is truly important in this world
Lord, he needs you
He is a good man no matter what has happened in his life
I truly believe that he is
For I have seen his heart
Lord, please give him another chance
Do not abandon him, Lord
Lord, help him see that you have forgiven him
Lord, show him that you are the only way
Rescue him, Lord, from this life of sin
From my heart and soul I pray for this miracle
Thank you, Lord, for listening to my humble prayer

When Doubts and Troubles Come My Way

When doubts and troubles come my way
I lift up my head to the sky and pray
I pray that he can make me strong each day
to handle each worry in my life
to give me the strength to be an assertive woman of God
I pray for patience but I think I have gained enough
I pray for wisdom
Then how many trials and tribulations come my way?
I pray for understanding that I might be a vessel of fairness
Right and wrong
What's fair is fair
To choose between what is good or bad for me
to know that I can be an instrument of peace,
Lord, guide me in my life
that I can with my words touch other people's lives
to give a sign of hope
to give a sign of faith
to motivate to change
For I have been able to do for myself
A living example I have become
to let others know that through salvation
my life has changed
I am not the same woman I was three years ago
I know that my body is my temple
Respect myself and respect other people's views
Be an example of what you have done to me
I am not perfect; I still have my good and bad days
of thinking, is it really worth it?
Doubts and fear come to me, leaving me feeling hopeless
But then again I pray to you for guidance constantly
For I know that every day is a test of life
I must choose right or wrong
I must be a living example
of the beauty of having been saved
and let my spirit grow
soar to a new outlook
of spirituality

307

Lord, What Can I Do?

Lord, what can I do
if all that I have loved is gone?
For once in my lifetime, I gave myself in heart and soul.
The love I thought I found, I lost.
The man whom I love is no longer close by.
My heart and mind he owns but does not acknowledge it, and why?
In my mind the memories linger and reoccur with visions of our
moments together.
I can't explain but his face I still could see in my mind as clear as day.
His smile I can't forget, the sound of his laughter I still hear.
His warmth and sweet caresses I still feel.
I ask, why? Why can I still keep him in my heart and mind?
Why does he trouble my heart with worries if he is okay?
Why do I still feel when he is in pain,
wondering about his well-being and how he is doing?
Can't stop thinking of how much I would have wished to share my life
with him,
of how beautiful it would have been for us to be together.
The peace and tranquility I once felt in his arms I miss dearly.
How much I share our interesting conversations,
the silliness of our playfulness together.
The memories are still bright and vivid like it was just yesterday he and I
were together.
The memories of the sea still clear, breezy wind, smell of sea salt in the
air I feel.
What a wonderful time I had with my soul mate that day,
fishing and close to nature all in the same way,
caressing his hair until he fell asleep in my arms,
sweetness surrounding us in the midst of the night,
the warmth and comfort I felt in his arms.
So peaceful a feeling I felt that I knew it was pure and real.
I knew we were meant to be,
for it happened as natural can be.
No effort, no pretending, no inhibitions, just pure love in its perfection in
action.
How I miss my soul mate.
How I wish I could see him.
How I yearn to be close to him.

How I wish I could see him again.
How I wish he could believe it's me whom his heart needs.
How I wish he could believe it's me whom his mind needs to challenge.

It's me who could be his partner and share his uniqueness.
It's me who loved that difficult man he says he is.
It's me who knows everything about him but still loves him.
It's me who accepts his past with no conditions,
proud to have share those precious moments with him.

It's me who accepts and is willing to tell the whole world that I love him
and I am not ashamed.
Proud to know that I love this man.
Proud to let others know that I am faithful only to him.
Proud to let others know how I still hope and have faith that my soul
mate will return.

Know him so well, love him for himself
not for what he can give me or take
but what we can both give to each other too.
To learn to grow in life and work out our differences is no mistake.
To learn to share the load together and bring blessings to our future.
To learn to accept that there are ups and downs but I will be happy as
long as he is around.
To learn to accept that his space is his at times, but mine is mine as well.

Forgive me for not knowing how to keep or challenge a man.
I was not taught what tricks to play, for I was raised so simple minded
that I did not think it would have mattered.
I do not know how to play those mating games, but I know how to love
with all my heart and soul.
I know that I love myself enough to be able to love others and also my
soul mate; that is true love in it's course.
Learn from mistakes: So what if I had children in the past? What
differences does it make if I was married before? Why think that matters
enough to keep you from your partner?
Why reject me because of pridefulness?
Try to forget me, but in your mind the memories still linger on....
I was the one good soul you let go ...
too blind to see that it was me you always wished for.
But you are still waiting for a trophy of a woman

who will be your display for others to see.
But the emptiness will still be there.
Somehow you will always wish it was me.
For to be happy, it is not the exterior that matters.
It's the heart and soul,
the patience and tolerance,
understanding and caring,
unconditional love and sharing.
Partners in life.
Partners in love.
Partners in spirit.
Partners in joy.
Partners in tears.
Partners in all:
that is what all your life you have needed but couldn't find;
you had it in front of your face and lost it in the search.

Thanking God

I thank God that I met you, for you helped me see what I needed to do
with my life
You do not know how amazing it has been, our paths crossing
For me it was not a mistake, my friend, it was meant to be
You and I were destined to meet, share our souls,
And learn some important things in life

I hope that I was able to contribute to your life like you have done to
mine
I am so much happier now; I cannot begin to explain
For you helped me see the way
And I was also able to see the way you needed to go
Amazing as it sounds, I am at peace and so very blessed to have had you
in my life
Although for a very short time, I found my best friend in life
The man I hoped I could share my life with for the very first time
The man who was my other half, my partner, my friend, and companion
for life

This doesn't happen too often, so I consider myself blessed
That I was able to share with the love of my life
Although so brief a moment in time
You gently stole my heart and mind
My soul you had long ago, for we were meant to be
You still cannot understand how I felt your pain

My love, I know so much about you that no one has been told
For the Spirit sees everything and God brings it to light
You see, I did not reject you; I could have if I wanted to
But I accepted you and felt so much pain and sorrow
That my heart could not contend with it, for I experienced what you had
experienced
And I know you so well

Strange as it sounds, I know you; you do not have to tell
For a spiritual connection is stronger than any physical attraction, as you
know
Many women you will find in your path

Either with more beauty or money, wealth, or materialism
But none will ever fit in my shoes

For none will be as beautiful as me
For my beauty comes from the heart
My mind is pure and my love comes from God
Yes, they will make you content temporarily
They will, but as time goes by, you see ...
That the space of emptiness in your heart will still be there
Because none will make you happy
Because the happiness comes from God
And being with the person God intended to help you grow spiritually
That is the secret my friend
Even though I will never get to see you in my life ever again
I hope to God that you find him and find true joy and happiness
These are the sincerest wishes for my best friend

Life Brings Many Changes

I have changed because my life has changed
I am more assertive than before, more conscious of my inner self
Than when I was twelve; I know that I have reached a peak
A peak in life that brings peace and tranquility
For I have decided to let go of all
I have found that my spirit is more important to invest in
Rather than waste my time on earthly things
For I am preparing myself for a bigger and greater change
The change to become a whole person spiritually
For God has come in my heart, and a new person I have become
No need to dwell on the past, for he has forgiven me
And I have forgiven them
No need to feel sorry for the things I could have done
For he knows I have tried my best in spite of everything life gave
I know that change is good; life brings many changes
I am ready to accept a new beginning as well
For here I am a changed woman
Free to understand that life brings many changes
And I am the proof of it....

Faith

To have faith is to sacrifice your needs for the needs of others.
It is to believe without seeing, touching, or having something physically
there
but your heart tells you soon it will be there!
To know that you love in secret and pray
for that special someone to willingly come your way;
by faith I have made the decision to love you.
I love you enough for the both of us.
At first I did not think to love you nor wanted to be tied down.
Yet at that time I did not know you were the one for me.
However, I fell in love with you indeed.

Please understand that I am trying very hard to let you go.
I am fighting to forget you.
I am in a constant battle with my heart and mind trying to deny that I
love you.
I have to let you go; that is why you do not hear from me any longer,
out of respect for your life and decisions you must make.
Let me tell you it is not easy for me; I love you too much to forget.
I can't forget those wonderful moments we shared together,
Your warmth, your touch, your smell, and your caresses.
I still sense you near; I yearn for you so much
that I cry myself to sleep almost every night.
It's like part of me is missing.
I wish you could understand the feeling.
It's so hard to explain, but, my friend, you probably will know one day.

I miss you so much that lately my heart cannot bear the ache.
For my best friend, you entered my heart unexpectedly
and your departure has left me questioning why you left.
Are you so cold hearted that the truth you cannot tell me face to face?
For I know that I meant so much more to you.
Is it because if you were to see me in person
the feelings would be rekindled and you would feel the closeness we
felt?
Your mind will realize the answers
and your soul will witness it all.
For you and I, no matter how different and far away we really are,

we are meant to be as one.
A bond exists that I cannot overlook,
a beautiful experience that I cherish in my heart—it will always be.
For I came in touch with my soul mate, but he did not find me.
A faded picture exists with a space for you to fill.

I know that you are not ready, and at least that is what you think,
or maybe it is that you are too proud to admit you care about me.
Look, I know that there will be many others who will come your way,
for in honesty, purity, and in kindness I gave myself to you.
Let me tell you that I am not one of your trophies or your picture-perfect
girlfriend.
Ask your photographic memory if it can recall me....
I am the one that shared the sea with you one day,
who spent the most amazing days in front of the universe.
Ask the sea, ask the sky, and ask the many creatures of the ocean
who witnessed our special moments we experienced together.
Remember the giant turtle who blessed us as she swan by
and went peacefully on her way?
The peace and tranquility we felt together during those days,
the warmth and perfect harmony we shared;
I can't forget how we went fishing and caught so many fish
as a blessing for the fondness that was coming our way.
It was such a great moment to share that part of me with you.
I know that we can spend so many more days
in the future if you have the courage to return.
For we are like childhood friends, so comfortable with each other.
So take my hands in your hands.
Let your heart take the lead.
Let your mind be set free,
for you and I were meant to be.

It does not make any difference to me what has happened to you in the
past.
I have accepted you just the way you are.
Meet me here in the present.
I will not judge you or reject you.
The distance and separation between us that is now keeping us apart
can only make us want each other more, for it is in the distance that the
heart grows fonder

and love grows deeper.
If we can stand the test of time and distance
then one day we can come together like nothing ever happened,
start fresh, and get to know each other better.
For we will have let go of all the flaws in our characters
that have interfered or that have come between us,
for that is how I feel now.
Don't give up on me.
Come share your future with me.
Seek me out and don't risk losing me because of pride.
You will see what I mean
and happiness will never leave our home,
for love will always be the welcome sign on our door....

Let Go, Let God

Let go of all the misery inside your heart
Let loose all of the resentment
Let go of all the grudges
Let go of all the pain
Let go of all the anger
Let go of all the bad memories
Let go of all the past that haunts you

Let God remove all misery
Let God remove all resentment
Let God remove all grudges
Let God remove all pain
Let God remove all anger
Let God erase bad memories
Let God give you a new life as a present

With God, you have true joy
With God, you do not hold grudges
With God, you do not hold on to pain
With God, you learn to be patient
With God, you gain good memories
With God, you do not fear the future
With God, all things are possible
With God, all dreams come true
With God, your life is positive
With God, you can gain insight
With God, your life is changed
With God, you make amends with your enemies
With God, you learn to love

Through His grace we are saved, with His love we are blessed
Through His suffering at the cross, we were spared spiritual death
Leave your pain, suffering, and baggage at the foot of the cross
Remember that He one day carried it for you and died in order for you to
be reborn
His sacrifice inspires hope; He loved us more than anyone will ever love
us

For He died for me and you
Through His death, we been saved
Through salvation, we have a chance to change

<u>Here Today, Gone Tomorrow</u>

We are here today and gone tomorrow
Your body is made up of flesh, spirit, and soul
Your flesh returns to the earth where it came from and was formed
Your spirit is God brethren; returns to the heavens
Your soul is eternal, waits for the day of judgment
To be judged if you will be going to heaven or to hell

We are here on earth for a purpose
Our flesh and human spirit leads us to life's consequences
Which are not of spiritual growth
Define what's good and what is evil
Human nature seeks to please the desires of the flesh

But your soul divines consciousness
Warns you to evaluate those mistakes
A chance to return back to your spiritual uniformity
To connect back to God the creator
Whose love is merciful and forgiving

Learn to reach the purpose of your life
To know that we are here but will be gone tomorrow
But your soul will live for all eternity
Your spirit is guided by the Holy Spirit
To teach you to seek inside your soul
For answers to what's right and what's wrong

That God is closer than you think and can imagine
Inside you are the answers to many questions
A creator has made you in His image
Seek Him with all the attention He deserves
Insight in life and outlook you will gain
Lessons in life that are sure to give you wisdom
Similarly life is a journey of spiritual gain
To know what you are here for
Is a deliverance from the monotony of life

The real reason for which you were born
The magic formula to your happiness
God is love and love is God
True freedom comes from being in touch with God
True living is knowing where you are in life
We are here today
And gone tomorrow
But with Christ there is eternal life

Lessons

Life lessons can come in many forms and in many ways
You can go through simple lessons and not experience much distress
Or, on the other hand, experience extensive lessons which cause great
trauma
Hard lessons in life make us wiser
Hurtful lessons make us stronger

Rejection by people is painful
But to know that God never leaves our side
Is all I ever need
You can be happily married at one point or another
Then all of sudden your partner dies

You can have a beautiful child
Who you loved and cared for
Unexpected causes can take him or her away

To love someone so deeply
Then lose them
Is pain unimaginable
But a lesson to grow from
You never know what comes out of it

There are times when this lesson
Brings forth great results
Turn the mishaps around into something positive
Then through your own lesson
You will be teaching others
And touching other people's lives

Lessons to build character
Lessons to build patience
Lessons to teach how to love
Lessons to learn how to cope
Lessons to teach others
Lessons which inflict pain
Lessons which make us cry
Lessons in which we feel as though we have died

Lessons that bring us joy
Lessons that help us find our souls
Lessons that lead us into real happiness
Lessons that teach us the real meaning of suffering

Remember that in every life lesson you go through
There is wisdom, character, and integrity to gain
For each life lesson brings us closer to God

Why Do You Have to Forgive?

Why do you have to forgive?
In order to be set free
To be what you have been set out to be
You must forgive and forget

Forgiving is hard to do, although it is so easy to cause someone pain
It's difficult to say I am sorry
To people we think we hate
My trespassers
My offenders
My abusers
My enemies
I know I must forgive and forget

If you reflect on the story of Joseph
And how his brothers did him wrong
They let themselves grow with envy and jealousy
And sold their brother to the highest bidder
After years went by and Joseph's life had been blessed
He was exalted because he forgave
Long before he met his brothers again
The power of forgiveness can open the road to freedom
And God can bless our lives if we learn just how to forgive and forget

On the other hand, in the story of Saul
A king who once was sanctified
His bitterness and envy hardened his heart with hatred
He conquered cities and in his power-seeking heart
Took everything that was in his path
He could not see himself forgiving his enemy
Instead vengeance was in his hands
The anger and power struggles
Instead created fear inside his mind
He could not bring himself to forgive
Only wretchedness he felt in his spirit

Nor did he accept others who expressed it
David forgave him, although he persecuted him
But Saul grew more infuriated
Premeditated David's death over and over again

Jesus is the finest example of forgiveness
He was tortured, mocked, and killed
And still he forgave us
His love, compassion, and mercy
Tell the greatest story ever told
For he died for us and took the blame
In silence he suffered for all humanity
Still in his last words ...
He whispered, "God forgive them, for they do not know what they do"
Forgiveness in its purest response
Forgiveness made the biggest difference for all of us
For Jesus is my example of how to forgive

I have forgiven my past
I have forgiven my trespassers
I have forgiven myself
I have forgiven my mistakes
I have forgiven my abusers
I have forgiven life wholeheartedly

For I have found the greatest love of all from beginning to end
Jesus had forgiven me perfectly
Jesus forgave my sins
That day he died in the cross for me
Gave me another chance to start anew
A blank slate
Love so overwhelming
That I can't put it in plain words
Forgiveness is healing
I feel brand new again
Reborn into forgiveness
My Jesus, he forgives and forgets

Judgment Day

1

If you died are you prepared to see your maker face to face?
Are you aware that this day will come no matter if you believe or not?
Have you thought about the things you want to say to Him?
Are you ready to meet your God personally as a judge?
How will you defend yourself during Judgment Day
When all the evidence will come into play?
Your life will be shown up in the skies
Like a movie playing on a big screen
All the sins will come to light

Are you prepared to explain the why and how?
Do you think just living life without a doubt
Will guarantee you an excuse that day?
Have you thought about your life on earth?
Rethink your existence and what was planned out

Did you ignore the voice of the Lord
Questioning His existence with prideful doubt?
Did you think that living in sin and ignoring Him will hide your
disobedience ?
Plead the fifth, no comments on that day
The Book of Life records it all word for word, action for action
Without question all will be disclosed
Every second, every minute, every hour, every day, every month,
Every year, and every chapter is still being written

How will you defend the evidence?
No lawyer from this earth will be able to help you then
No Johnny Cochran or no famous lawyer will be able to match up
To the presence of the Almighty God
Except unless you have examined your life
And
Realize that the only way your sins will be cleared
Is to accept Jesus as your Lord and Savior
Defending you for the price He paid at the cross for your sins
Sins forgotten
Records sealed

2

Imagine having the best lawyer in the world
Jesus, the greatest defense lawyer, representing you
He will be right next to your side
Presenting your life
Telling God the judge
"My sacrifice has paid the price
Lord, have mercy, for he is washed by the Blood of the Lamb
Through My sacrifice at the cross
His sins are all forgiven
Wiped out clean"
The Lord will look to His son Jesus and say
Welcome him, Son, into Our Kingdom

Think about all the possibilities
If your lawyer is Satan the accuser
Who knows very well all of your past mistakes
A wicked witness to all your sins
He has always been around to tempt you
He will bring out all the evil accounts
With a prideful grin between his teeth
He will state, "His soul belongs to me"
No chance will you have to even defend yourself around him
Nor will you have a chance to repent of your sin
When you know quite well you gave into sins
When in your life on earth you kept ignoring God's word
Telling yourself I don't believe it! Nonetheless,
There is no heaven! There is only hell on earth

Continuing on your sins you went
Hardened your heart instead
The devil wrote in his book
"Another soul I have just won!"
He'll spend eternity in hell
What will you say when your name is called on Judgment Day?

The Different Faces at Christmas

I see the face of a destitute homeless man who waits in an alley, cold and hungry, covered with cardboard and no place to go. His blanket is an old newspaper and rags which he has collected from the local dump. He has never had the pleasure of feeling the warmth of a fireplace or of a place he can call his own. I wonder how he will celebrate Christmas, if at all.

I see the face of a fragile woman dying of AIDS, with tubes in her nose to assist with the breath of life, longing for air as the minutes go by. Feeling lonely and helpless, she waits, and finally succumbs to her death. Without a breath left she says good-bye cruel, cruel world.... This Christmas I pray that a cure can be found and that no one else will die such an agonizing death!

I see the face of a small child who, at the hands of his loved ones, only experiences pain. With his small hand covering his face as he gently weeps, he says, "Please don't hit me, don't hit me, I won't do it again!" I pray that this Christmas they can spare him the shame of being hit and tortured by those very same hands, the hands that were meant to protect him and shield him when he is afraid.

I see the face of a lonely stranger who never has known love, and with all of his heartfelt hope he wishes for a miraculous kind word from another that will bring joy! So simple a wish to hope for, what we take for granted, mere words we ignore! At this Christmas may the angels comfort you with loving kindness, and protect and guide you when you are feeling all alone!

I see the face of an addict in an empty lot who shoots up his system to numb all of his life's pain. He is hoping one day to stop so that he will no longer remember all of his life's suffering; then it will not be in vain. I wish for him that this Christmas will be the last time, "The last time this addict decides to use and hope that he can begin—begin a new life without drugs."

I see the face of a man whose life's sorrows and misfortune have driven him to drinking. Drowning in alcohol are all his fears, troubles, misery, and despair. He is determined to finally forget once and for all the bad choices he has made! I hope that this Christmas this man can find out and accept that in life we all make mistakes; this is what being human is all about. I hope he can see that God can forgive us, even if others don't know how! Then how come is it so hard to forgive ourselves as well?

I see the face of a woman who gets abused every day at the very same hands of the one she thought loved her and who promised to protect her till death do us part. I see that she lives her life in disorder every day, wishing one day it would stop, and that she can escape alive, if she only can. I pray that this Christmas her wish can come true and she can finally leave this treacherous man and be able to stand on her own two feet. May love finally touch her and help soothe her pain, the pain caused by the man she thought was her best friend.

I see the face of a prostitute who deeply believes that she has to sell her body to make up for the love and support that her father never gave! She is scarred by the consequences of childhood abuse, feeling unwanted, and misused! She takes drugs to help numb all the memories, all the memories of the circumstances she had to endure when she was only the tender age of eight. My wish is that this Christmas you will finally see that our Heavenly Father has watched over you from up above and has always loved you, even though others have expressed nothing! God says that it is never too late to change from a crooked path and just turn around and walk in a straight way.

I see the faces of those who are mentally ill, locked up in a ward with only blank walls to stare at, drugged up by the potion that should be helping instead. Their lives go by not knowing which day it is, growing old with despair, waiting for the day a once familiar face can say, "You are loved in spite of it all"—I hope that this Christmas you can become healthy mentally and understand that you are not at fault and that your sickness is not a punishment but a mystery of life that we cannot question because we are not GOD.

I see the face of a child with no parents at all, who anxiously waits in foster care. He dreams of two parents who will take him in and show him the love that he has never seen—with no guarantee that the next family will be the perfect parents he wishes they could be. He still takes the chance because having new parents is better than none! I pray that every child without parents will be lucky enough to find two loving people who will especially care to raise him in patience, love, and acceptance, the ingredients of life that can guarantee a healthy adult!

I see the many different faces at Christmas with faith, hope, and love. "Do not despair!" says the Lord. "I am the only assurance in life you will need; I will bring you peace, love, and strength to carry on!" Merry Christmas to those many different faces who long in one way or another for those precious little things we often take for granted and that they can only hope for! This Christmas remember those suffering faces less fortunate than you, be thankful for what you have, and pray for those who do not!

The Year of My Blessings

This coming year will be the year of my blessings;
in victory I claim it,
for God has heard my prayers
I listen to his answers through
many individuals who have shared a special message with me
They have told me that God has listened, and He will bless me greatly
For I have gone through a metamorphosis of changes,
many changes which He intended personally for me
to bring me into reality and let me see the light within

Bring forth a new beginning
and set a spirit of hope
He has shown me to be patient
and appreciate everything I experience
For He knows the lessons I needed to go through in order to grow
spiritually
God has shown me to have faith no matter how bleak my life may seem
He has been my comfort when no one was around
For He is my guiding light, showing me which way to go
It is in the Lord's time, not mine
God has a specific process in which I must be refined
For I was not yet prepared to reach the momentum
I needed to bring to memory all those disturbing hurts from the past
Renounce all negative feelings by calling them out by name
I needed to let go of many hurtful memories
release all the pain that was buried in my heart
let go of all emotions and past history of abuse
let go of all the memories, let go of all anger
let go of all resentment and finally be set free
forgive all who treated me unfairly
forgive myself for being a prey
forgive the past memories
release them towards the wind
forgive myself for letting it happen
stop blaming and carrying the shame
He has forgiven them
and forgiven me as well
Forgive with all my heart all who caused me pain

take all of it out of my heart
be cleansed of my imperfections
Lord, I will confess my sins to you
I know that you have carried this burden on the cross
No one can carry pain but Jesus
and He is the only way

I believe I've been set free in hope
for a new future God has set out for me
I have finally become a new person by the lessons I have lived through
The old person is dead and buried along with all the memories
A new being has been transformed and a new woman I've become
For His love and mercy I am standing free to live
to become what He has set me to be

To bring forth all wondrous plans He has intended for me
I am a new woman who is not afraid to reach the highest goals
I will strive to be the best in all I do for Him
I will not worry about tomorrow or what I will need
for God knows what I need and He will supply for me

How amazing to be given a second chance in life
to be able to let go of all the baggage from the past
to live so free and just be me
to have a hope for a better future
because I know that God will be there for me
I have reached an enlightenment of peace and tranquility
no one has been able to give to me

Nothing in this world has been able to provide
the finest redemption to get rid of all my pain
For what I needed in my life was God's loving embrace
His total forgiveness
and His mercy
to let me see a brighter day

Lord, I am so grateful for letting me see the way
How blind I've been not to focus on You instead
I know now that if I want things to work out in every area of my life
I need to let You be my counselor and also be my guide
I don't want to make any more mistakes again

I want to make smart choices with your approval first
in everything I do and what I choose to do
Lord, You will be first so that Your blessings will come forth
And if others cannot accept me as I am nor for who I have become
then it is their loss, not mine
For I am valued in the heavens
and my father is the King of the Universe
My God, He has accepted me
What else do I need?

My Interview with an Eighty-Year-Old Lady

I had the blessing to interview an eighty-year-old lady
Whom I asked, "What is the most important thing in life?"
To which she answered, "Your relationship with God"
I kept probing and probing
Looking for other answers
Not mother, father, children, money, or wealth
None were seen as the most important thing
"God is the answer
In everything I seek"
She answered
She then stated
That "love is also important because God is love
Love forgives
Show it
Practice it
Live it"

To see if her answers would change I asked:
"If you have anything to change in your life what would it be?"
Instead this old lady firmly stated:
"I don't think I would do anything different
Except to have become a teacher and been educated
Life has been fruitful for me"
She also mentioned that in life
"You have to trust God and He will direct your path"

Here I was thinking that this old lady had found the secret to life
She knew that in her life she lived the best way possible
By worshipping God in everything she had done
To me she was the best teacher
One could have ever found
For not having an education
Much wisdom she had expressed
The best advice if any
Given with a smile on her face

333

I kept wondering how come she was so happy
Her smile never left her face
She giggled and laughed out loud
Like a young child
No apparent wrinkles to link her to her age
Her face was like an angel
Waiting to gain her wings in heaven

I went on to ask her what were her feelings about growing old?
To which she replied:

"When you get old, you want to be closer to God,
Do things that are pleasing in His sight
Pretty soon you will be with Him in paradise
Thank God for life; I have no pain
I have been blessed

"Right now I look forward to going to paradise
With Jesus who died for me"

I asked her why was she so happy
She said: "When you worship God
There is a peace of mind that never leaves you
Because you have His peace when anything comes up
He gives you the courage and faith to overcome it

"In my old age He has given me grace to keep going
Eventually everyone gets old
One important thing is to accept growing old
I see people who I know who get old and are afraid to be old
They are scared about the future
When God is in your heart there is peace like no other
And you look forward too seeing him sooner"

I was running out of time
And asked her my last question
What did she recommend to learn about life?
"Trust God and lean not to your own understanding"

This was coming from an individual with
Eighty years of life experience
To which she acknowledged no regrets
But acceptance, love, and gratitude
That God has let see another day
Even though she looks forward to
Being in heaven each day

I felt as though I had found the fountain of youth
To know that we can look forward to eternal life in heaven
"That is the secret to living life on earth"
And this ends my spritiual journey....

Another Year and Another Chapter

<u>Another Year Has Passed</u>

And still I yearn to be with you
I have been faithful and true to you
Always hopeful that one day
You would come back in my direction
I pray and I pray for God to steer you
And finally show you the way to my heart and mind
Still I wait …
For a response to your silence
Never knowing if I am ever in your thoughts
Hoping that the memories have never left you
What we shared was real
It was beautiful
Peace and serenity we both found in each other

Those days of togetherness
I still relive—just like yesterday I was in your arms
Watching you sleep
Feeling your warmth
What I felt that very moment next to you
I will not regret
Nor would I want to forget
That is what love is all about

Something so strong but so simple
Connection was there mentally, spiritually, and physically
What else was needed?
But then again there was a bondage weighing you down
Pulling you away
As if tied with a rope
It pulled and pulled
Until it swayed and swayed you away

Fear, intimidation, and unrealistic expectations
Sent you in a frenzy of disbelief
That what happened could not be
Your selfishness kept you busy at all times
Not to even have a chance to rethink of me
Or allow me into your heart and mind

Suffering, sadness, and turmoil exits
I would be feeling the same thing
My love, I know that you are not happy
You are walking on empty
There is a void deep within your spirit
I feel what you're feeling
The storm of stress
The perfectionist in you
Reality is escaping you
Deep down, those wounds are bleeding
Seeping hurt from the past
You have not yet allowed healing
Due to the anger in your heart
Numb it with artificiality
Forgetting it in reality
Not accepting the pain
Not letting go of it
Nor forgiving yourself

My love, how can I make you understand
That this fight I fight with you?
Every night I pray to God
To heal your broken heart
And mine
To make you a brand-new man
The one you are meant to be
The amazing man I have seen
Beyond what you have even dared to examine

I saw the real you and I love you for you

Do You Remember Me?

The laughter and sincerity in my smile
The glow of my eyes stared at you deeply
Beauty inside and out
I led you in but you stopped dead in your tracks
For fear of intimacy
Froze you in space

Your mistaken view of what a real women is
Do you know what it takes to fit in my shoes?
Can you see past the hurt inside?
Can you see the clarity of my soul?
That joy in me that little things make me so happy
You don't even have to try hard
Companionship
Trust
Attention
Warmth
Sharing
Love
That is all I need

No need for richness, glamour, or superficiality
Things are temporary
Things lose luster
Things get taken away
What I want is something permanent
Something lasting
Something true
Friendship
Companionship
Relationship

Friends
Lovers
Partners
In life

Commitment: what is it?
Commitment is respecting
Sharing
Communicating
Discussing
Challenging
Appreciating
Understanding
Recognizing
Strength
Values
Morals
Goals
Spiritual growth

In life love has to be nourished
Agreement by both partners
To make it work
Finding resolutions to problems
Finding answers even when it seems impossible
Working together for a better life
Two make things work well if you try

We will be blessed
If you decide to learn how to love
Learn how to share
Learn how to appreciate
Truthful
I have always been
Know that you need someone like me
To help you become accountable
That life is better when we share
With someone who truly cares

Let's come together in truth
Let's come together for growth
Let's come together with respect
Let's come together with dedication to make it work

Don't need much
Just an open mind and heart
Let me show you
Let me guide you
Let me teach you how
My love is pure and simple
You will know my intentions
Were always pure

But there is no mistake between us
We are two of a kind
Born for each other
You will see that I am not wrong.
The answers you will find in time
God is in the plan
We will do great things together
Trust me
I have never been so confident
That this is as good as is gets
For the love in my heart for you
Has been God given

Yesterday I Was Observing

How quickly life goes by
Years just keep passing
As fast they can
Like a movie
Being fast-forwarded

Scenes and memories
Quickly, briskly, and swiftly
Are starting to fade away
That is how it looks like
Like
A feather flying by in the sky

Down with the old
In with the new
Things have changed
Nothing stays the same
Infant is born
A child is raised
A teenager is grown
An adult has matured
In old age we reach wisdom
To death we finally succumb

Do you remember when your child
Said their first words?

Do you remember when your child lost his first tooth?
Do you remember when your teenager learned to drive or had their first
date?
Do you remember as an adult the best years of your life?
What was important then?
What made you happy?
Was your life complete?
Did you reach your goals?
Or did you remember
What was the most important thing in life?

Did you forget that you would get old?
They say in old age you can reach wisdom?
That is if you have accepted your life as is
That is if you have learned to forgive
That is if you have learned what is joy?
A wise person is one who learned from their mistakes
Live to tell
Live to teach
Live to warn
Live to show what real love is
If only you have knowledge of it
Can you show it?
The ultimate selfless act of loving others
When you truly love yourself enough to know you
Only then you can say, "I am wise in my old age"

What is Self-Obsession?

What is self-obsession?
It is the self-centeredness never outgrown?
Your wants and needs become demands
When things don't go your way
Anger strikes out of your psyche
Contentment, fulfillment, and love
Are impossible
For nothing can fulfill the emptiness in your heart
The void becomes a self-obsession
Insanity strikes thinking of the past again and again
Denial and unrealistic expectations
Is this how you deal with issues?

Resentment, anger, and fear
Is how you react
But why?
The child psyche has not ever grown up
The adult is still a child
The inner child is what they call it
But in reality it is self-obsession
A fantasy world is how you live
Denial of reality is how you perceive
How you think, feel, and react to people, places, and things

What you need is
Acceptance, love, and faith
Acceptance of your past
Forgiveness of your pain
Learn to love and give love
Learn to accept your lot in life
Be acquainted with yourself
Before you form an opinion of someone else
Do not get angry when things
Do not turn out the way you expected

Self-fixation, self-centeredness, self-loathing
The inner child is a narcissistic personality
Thinking only of "I"

Loving yourself too much is idolatry
Sinful nature, seeking pleasure
The only relief that you can think of
Is numbing the reality of your life
Leaving you alone in your own high
Lost in a fantasy land
Where feelings, emotions, and spirituality don't exists
But a desensitization of an individual
Who becomes disassociated?
Mind weak
Allows the darkness to creep in
Negative only exists
Haunting you
To keep you cornered in a world of disbelief
No morals, guidance, or higher power to seek
Only your self-obsession
That is what you believe

But you know …
That there are possibilities
There is healing
By the higher power
The darkness can become light
If you believe in Him

The self-obsession can become
Self-giving, humbleness, and conviction
That the power of faith can overcome fear
The power of love can become a miracle
The power of hope can overcome all the negatives
The power of God
Can provide you with a blank slate to start with
Self-obsession no longer will exist
But a new you
With hope, faith, and love
All things can be possible
Through a higher power

Learning about Life

I learned about life through
Trials and errors
Lessons no one ever told me anything about
No one ever warned me
That they could happen
I did not have someone to guide me
A manual I never found
All I knew was to do the best I could

I tried hard even when I failed at times
I cried the tears of pain
I wiped them dry
And lifted my head up high
Prayed and prayed

My heart has known many
Rejections
Suffering
And deceptions
But I have learned to forgive
And forget
Keep on walking the journey
Without dismay
Forget the past
Hope for a better future

These things I learned about life
Those without faith, hope, and love
They are nothing
They walk alone in life
However
Love can conquer all
Faith can move mountains
Hope can give you strength
To face your life realities
Essentials for your journey in life
Needed to make your journey safe
Guidance to lead you in the right path

Love to let the light shine
True joy is what you will find
If you learn these principles
Early on in life....

Stillness of Time

I have known isolation and I have known companionship
The times of isolation I learned about myself
The times of companionship I learned about others
With time I learned to believe in myself
In time companions come and go

I had experience fear
but now I have know bravery
I once feared getting old
In the present time I accept it with courage
In my younger years I felt as time was moving slowly
I have mature and it seems as time flies swiftly

I could not stop time when experiencing troubles
It seems during those moments time was at a stop sign
The happy memories went as fast as they came
No chance to savor the moments
or forget the regretful stages
For time is just a moment in space

It seems as it was just yesterday
My oldest son was born
Just looking into his eyes
Made my eyes glow
Watch him grow so quickly
Pre-school started
High school ended
College begun
Boy has he grown

I can not say that I can remember every single moment
He made me smile
Times when he got sick
And the times when he was alright
The same happen when my second son was born
By the third son I learned that pictures tell a thousand stories
Soon there after my fourth son was born
Again I took out the camera
Made sure that time can be capture in a photograph

But time will not change the love I have experienced
Nor the love I have for them
I love them all more than yesterday
For in time I have learned patience
Within time I have learned peace
In time I have found myself
In time I took the heed
For I realized that you have to set goals over time
For you can not beat time
Trying to accomplish all you can in a nick of time

For time will soon be passing
But instead of time moving slowly
I will be the one in slow motion
For time will pass so quickly
When I reflect to look back
Time has already past
The only thing I will have with me
Will be the memories of the times

For time did not stop for me
Nor was I able to stop time
It beat me in the race
Even when I ran as fast as I can
The ending soon will come
This will be the end of time for me

I reached a milestone trying to figure out
How much I can do with my time
Who will remember me in time?
Will I be forgotten with time?
Or will time then be in a standstill
Death they claim is the end of time
Will this be the end of me?
Or will time bless me with cherished memories

For those whom I loved time will continue on
For those who have hated me time will drag
For time is just an instantaneous moment in life
As soon as we are born we age

Time rolls from the first cry
Continues to the last cry
For time will not stop for you or me
Time is everlasting …..

Life is full of surprises

Just when you think that you have adjusted
Minor disruptions happens
Set backs keeping you in line with life
Humbling your soul to be guided
Trying to catch your attention
To what is really important
Focusing on what could happen
Instead what already has happened?
Teaching you that some things will never happen
Warning you against those things that should not happen
Instinct inside deep within your spirit
becomes restless
A voice telling you no it is not suppose to happen
Be careful, be cautious and be guarded
For you never know the pain it may cause you

Still I insist of only seeing outside of the box
I still perceive
To think that it is as nice as my eyes has seen
But inside the box
What can it be?
For deception, lies and manipulation
Disguise the beauty of the design
It looks so real
And wholesome
I sense that it can also be beautiful inside?
But what a mistake
Inside I only found lies
Shame, disgust and selfishness
I became saddened by what I seen
And left that box alone

A box is just an interpretation
Of what is inside of a selfish person
That those who pretend to have a great design
Thinking that it will never wrinkle
Nor make a mistake within lies
Their self loathe makes them think they are indestructible

And that everything is indispensable
"I am only in it for the game" they say
Past time for my pleasure
A good time for the night
One, two or three I will use and then discard
For their ugliness inside
Will soon be found and then what?
I ran and ran as far as I can
For they only exist for pleasure
A good time here or there
Different ones for each night
Who cares if they get sick?
As long as they get their gist

Despair, lowliness, and shame
Is what they will feel
When they look at in the mirror
For they have never been able to distinguish
Between what's real or what is fake
They can not see the beauty inside the box
Because what they seek is only for a good time
Keep on using and discarding
For one day someone will be sick of them
And discard them like a broken box
Inside the garbage shoot…

The Day the Earth Cried and the Sea Roared

The day like any other day in a beautiful vacation landscape
Islands of beautiful discoveries
Fantastic sceneries too magnificent to describe
The sea and beaches all so beautiful
The ocean in all majesty
But one day
Without no warning
The sea roared
Attack with a Tsunami

The sea roared in tempest waves
Covered the land without a haste
Swallowed whole everything in sight
Left no traces in the sands

The sea roared in mass destruction
Carrying lives into the ocean
Young and old were taken that day
Drowned within seconds
Not a chance for an S.O.S sign for help

The sea roared causing mass destruction
Destroying buildings, houses and huts
All that stands now is debris and parts of what used to be standing

The earth is weeping right now
Many thousandths will ceased to exists
From dust to dust they will become
No time for sorrow for much is to be done

The earth is weeping reminding us
That everyday there is a call from all creation
Earth, wind, skies and sea's
Are crying out
Come seek me please!
God is allowing them to invocate

A call of warning for all to hear
That the time is now for all to hear
God is calling the world to heed
Seek me now
Do not fear
Come back to me for there is hope
The earth is weeping and the sea is roaring
Listen closely
Creation needs to come closer to its beginnings
Spiritual closeness to the creator
For the sin is too much for the earth and sea to bear
The earth is weeping and the sea is roaring......
Listen to the sounds within your soul...

<u>Days gone by</u>

Yesterday was but a dream
The day when life was so much simpler
When remembering the days
My baby grew into a toddler
Speak his first words
"Momma"
My baby learned to walk today
He slightly bump his head
But still he looks at me so proud
And smile
He then forgot all about
His smile cure the blues if ever they were around
Yesterday feels like a dream
When ever I think of those days when the child
Who grew into a man?

Life was all about making sure
my children were all happy
Making sure that they were properly feed
Well taken care off each day
Clean clothes
Toys
And everything four boys can want

Yesterday was all but a dream
When life took me much farther it seems
Remembering days when I felt so loved
Seeing their smiles
Each day
Watching their first softball game
What a treat
The proudest mom around was me

Getting their uniforms clean and pressed
Caps, socks and helmet ready
Let's go play a game
My baby hit a home run today
He ran as fast as he could
He made momma so proud

Watching them grow
Seems like a dream
For it was just yesterday
I held them in my arms
And cuddled them
Wrapped in a blanket
Which I made especially for them

It seems like a dream
But yesterday was but a vision
Time has since long gone
Days are gone into yonder
Memories are like yesterday
Caught in a dream of reminiscences

Don't give your love away

Don't give your love away
to someone who won't care
Don't give away the best of yourself
Honor your temple and stay pure
Don't allow anyone to take from you
Without giving something back
Kisses, hugs, caresses
Is nothing if there is no love?
Is wasted intimacy
On unfilled

Love yourself enough
Not to fall into a trap
To fall in the arms of enticement
Wake up to an empty pillow
Not even a note or
Phone call
For he took
And you let him have it
He used
And then discarded
Only good for a one night stand
Hang around
He's taken you as a fool

It's a joke, he keeps a score board
Black book to keep it noted
This one I took for granted
No feelings or remorse
Just wasted time
Wasted laughs
Wasted kisses
Hugs
And caresses

On someone who doesn't deserve it
Leave you use and feeling worn
No regrets

Is this for real?
Thinking he will call you today
Minutes, hours becomes days
Still not a sign if he still alive

Where is he?
Does he care?
Does he even have a heart to know?
What's real?
Does he even know any remorse?

He is the deceiver manipulator
Who knows every trick in the book?
A hound for women
With good looks
Sexed them and leave them
Used them and discard them
What the hell!
Life is too short!
Enjoy many as they come and go
And so he says!

Does this man even realize?
That he is playing with emotions and lives
A player can not last for ever
For one day all his tricks will catch up to him
The lies
The silence
The avoidance
Manipulation
Fetish
Deception
Of
The life of a philandering man

Stand up
Answer back
What the cat got your tongue
Too scare to face the facts
Grow old
Sick

And
Lonely
For nobody
Will want a man who never tells the truth
Face yourself one day
Your wicked ways
Will end.....

I end this book with this procession
That in life dreams do come true
If you strive hard and fight to make it happen
At last I have finished this book
And with joy in my heart
I wish all the world can read it
To see beyond the writer words
See the heart and soul instead
To share God's love in its place
God Bless... Claribel Coreano

About The Author

A native of the Dominican Republic, Claribel Corcano is employed in the area of social services in Connecticut. Her goals are to complete her master's degree in psychology and social work and to establish her own practice. Her inspiration for writing has been the many challenges and experiences she has faced throughout her life. Her dream has always been to write a book and this has provided a unique motivation to express her feelings through poetry. Her hobbies include painting, writing, and cooking.

Printed in the United States
61279LVS00004B/1-21